The Creative Problem Solver

PEARSON

At Pearson, we believe in learning – all kinds of learning for all kinds of people. Whether it's at home, in the classroom or in the workplace, learning is the key to improving our life chances.

That's why we're working with leading authors to bring you the latest thinking and best practices, so you can get better at the things that are important to you. You can learn on the page or on the move, and with content that's always crafted to help you understand quickly and apply what you've learned.

If you want to upgrade your personal skills or accelerate your career, become a more effective leader or more powerful communicator, discover new opportunities or simply find more inspiration, we can help you make progress in your work and life.

Pearson is the world's leading learning company. Our portfolio includes the Financial Times and our education business, Pearson International.

Every day our work helps learning flourish, and wherever learning flourishes, so do people.

To learn more, please visit us at www.pearson.com/uk

The Creative Problem Solver

12 smart tools to solve any business challenge

Ian Atkinson

PEARSON

Harlow, England • London • New York • Boston • San Francisco • Toronto • Sydney
Auckland • Singapore • Hong Kong • Tokyo • Seoul • Taipei • New Delhi
Cape Town • São Paulo • Mexico City • Madrid • Amsterdam • Munich • Paris • Milan

PEARSON EDUCATION LIMITED
Edinburgh Gate
Harlow CM20 2JE
United Kingdom
Tel: +44 (0)1279 623623
Web: www.pearson.com/uk

First published 2014 (print and electronic)

ISBN: 978-1-292-01618-4 (print)
       978-1-292-01619-1 (eText)
       978-1-292-01620-7 (PDF)
       978-1-292-01621-4 (ePub)

British Library Cataloguing-in-Publication Data
A catalogue record for the print edition is available from the British Library

Library of Congress Cataloging-in-Publication Data
Atkinson, Ian.
  The creative problem solver : 12 smart tools to solve any business challenge / Ian Atkinson.
    pages cm
  Includes bibliographical references and index.
  ISBN 978-1-292-01618-4
  1. Problem solving. 2. Management. I. Title.
  HD30.29.A85 2014
  658.4'03--dc23
                        2014010991

10 9 8 7 6 5 4 3 2 1
18 17 16 15 14

Cover design by Rob Day

Print edition typeset in 9.5pt Scene by 30
Print edition printed and bound in Great Britain by Henry Ling Ltd, at the Dorset Press, Dorchester, Dorset

NOTE THAT ANY PAGE CROSS REFERENCES REFER TO THE PRINT EDITION

For Daisy Boo

Contents

PART III
INSPIRATION

About the author

Author of several bestselling business books, Ian Atkinson has had a varied career – as an award-winning copywriter, board-level creative director, acclaimed speaker, trainer and brand strategy consultant. He has a degree in psychology and an interest in the role behavioural science can play in marketing communications.

He's the founder of communications consultancy *Sodium* and has worked with some of the biggest brands in their sectors including Avis, B&Q, Barclays, Cow & Gate, Dyson, Jaguar, Lloyds, Macmillan, Nando's, National Geographic, Next, Oxfam, Sky, Stihl, The Royal British Legion, Toyota and Zurich.

Introduction

'If everybody is thinking alike, somebody isn't thinking.' GEORGE SPATTON

Pixar came up with the plots and main characters of *A Bug's Life*, *Monsters Inc.*, *Finding Nemo* and *WALL-E* in a single lunch meeting.

Films that went on to gross more than £1.5 billion. Dreamt up over lunch.

And it seems unlikely that, while slurping their half-caff, low foam, extra tall, skinny lattes with hazelnut syrup they were also wrestling with an A1 printout of a process flowchart entitled 'How to come up with great movie ideas'.

They didn't need to. Because successfully solving problems, seizing opportunities and innovating isn't about following a dry, dusty process. It's about being in the 'right frame of mind'. It's about thinking creatively.

Which highlights why traditional problem-solving models are often so ineffectual. Because instead of changing your thinking, they just replace your thinking.

Their series of steps and impressive-sounding acronyms might create a wonderful sense of being productive. And at the time, you really feel like you're *doing* something.

But afterwards, when the novelty wears off ... you see that all you're left with is the same old ideas you could have come up with in a half hour's traditional brainstorm. You realise you're no Pixar.

This book will change that for you.

It cuts through the acronyms and processes to reveal how to run rings around a problem. It looks at innovation, creativity, the way the brain works and the way people work in groups – and identifies the strengths and weaknesses of all those factors in problem-solving and innovation workshops.

But most of all, it gives you 12 tools. Simple, powerful, practical tools that will help you become brilliant at business problem solving and innovation – as an individual, a team and a business.

Because, as that Pixar lunch meeting showed, problem solving can be quick *and* powerful. It can be interesting *and* successful. And it doesn't have to feel like work to still work really well.

Problem solving solved

'There is nothing as powerful as an idea whose time has come.' VICTOR HUGO

The pub is packed. The bar is four deep, all elbows and attitude. You just want to get served and get back to your friends, a.s.a.p. Ideally, before someone nicks your chair.

But there's a problem. You've ordered three pints of Guinness.

The problem with Guinness is, it takes two minutes to pour a pint. You have to put some in (at a 45-degree angle), let it settle, then fill the rest up. What a pain. Compared to a pint of lager (or quicker still, a bottle of lager), it's something of a laggard.

Which rather puts people off. So if you're Diageo (the owner of Guinness), what do you do? How do you solve the problem of it taking a long time to pour?

By shifting perceptions. Instead of trying to develop 'Instant Guinness', they just position its slowness as a positive rather than a negative. With the slogan 'Good things come to those who wait'. Backed up with brilliant advertising like the *Surfer* TV ad, voted 'Best ad of all time' by the public in a survey by the *Sunday Times* and Channel 4.

A simple, surprising and elegant solution to a significant disadvantage Guinness appeared to have, compared to the competition. Now you're waiting at the bar not because Guinness is annoyingly slow. But because it's fantastically good, and worth waiting for.

As Winston Churchill said: 'We have no money, we shall have to think.'

And that's what this book is all about.

Why me

I studied psychology at university, which gave me a lifelong interest in the way the mind works. From optical illusions to cognitive biases to pattern recognition to the way our memory stores information, there's a lot in the popular psychology field to intrigue and inform without needing a NASA-sized brain to understand all the really clever stuff.

Then in my career I went on to become the creative director at several advertising and marketing agencies. Which is often all about creative problem solving – whether that problem is something that might seem pretty minor (like coming up with a witty slogan for an ad campaign), or something a bit more meaty (like how to reposition brand x, sell more of product y, or get customers to understand the value of service z). Whatever the problem, when you're a creative director part of the job is coming up with creative solutions.

So over the years I read about, or discovered, or developed, lots of different approaches for coming up with creative answers to challenging briefs.

And I realised that although what I was doing was 'being creative', I was also solving problems – and finding interesting ways to solve those problems. Because that's all a brief is, really: a problem in need of solving. A problem that can be solved more spectacularly with creative thinking.

Then I started doing the occasional problem-solving session with clients here and there, where I'd talk about how these creative thinking principles could work for them too, to solve real business problems (or seize on real business opportunities).

Refining those principles, using them 'in the real world' and seeing some tremendous success come from them – as well as recognising where other companies might have used similar approaches to achieve their success – they became the 12 tools in this book. Thinking tools with a creative pedigree that many clients have found a refreshingly energising, effective and jargon-free method for making leaps forward.

I hope that after reading the book you'll feel the same way.

Problems not puzzles

There are business problems that can be fixed with hard work, study and iteration. For the sake of distinction, let me call them puzzles. I could liken them to your car breaking down. Why has it stopped working? You know it can work – it just was, a moment ago. But now some part (or parts) of it has come loose or broken or got misaligned or overheated or worn out or run out of some vital fluid.

It's a puzzle: with some mechanical expertise (like that of, say, a mechanic) and a little time, the issue can be found. And then simply, precisely, perfectly fixed. A new spark plug (or whatever) and you're back on the open road, belting out *Bat Out of Hell* and wondering how on earth the appalling driver in front of you ever passed their test.

But many more business problems are not like that. There is no definite, logical, knowable answer. There are too many variables, too many unknowns and just too many interactions to be able to draw it all out like an equation and deduce that if you double x and halve y you'll achieve z.

This book is for all of those problems. All the ones beyond simple analysis and the (often misplaced) comfort of logic.

And that's important, because puzzles that can be solved through study and iteration are already being solved. All the time. By you and by your competitors. It's vital work, of course it is, but because those puzzles are solvable just by rigorous effort, and because their solutions appear risk-free (since they are, in theory, provable), everyone's doing them – and you'll never get ahead by just following the herd.

The 12 tools you'll read about are for bigger, messier, newer problems. Ones for which there doesn't seem to be a logical, provable answer. Ones which call for a bold leap, not a timid tiptoe.

Problems and opportunities

Despite the name, you don't have to use *The Creative Problem Solver* just for solving problems. After all, 'problem solving' suggests something has to go wrong before you act. There needs to be a problem to solve.

Which can mean you're spending your most creative time on fighting fires, not blazing new trails. And that can cost businesses a fortune – as the very best, most innovative and exciting tools for solving problems can also be excellent at helping you maximise opportunities.

In other words, the thinking tools that could have helped BP come up with more innovative and efficient ways to clean up the Deepwater Horizon oil spill could also have been the tools Apple used to develop the iPhone – a phone without physical keys at a time when the notion seemed ludicrous to the competition.

PROBLEM-SOLVING TIP

Problem ... or opportunity? Hundreds of years ago, two salesmen were sent to a small African nation by a shoe manufacturer to check out the market's potential. The first salesman came back saying, 'No, there's no potential there – nobody wears shoes.' Whereas the second salesman came back saying, 'Yes, there's huge potential there – nobody wears shoes.'

Sometimes we'll look at how a tool can be used for innovation as well as for problem solving, but not every time as that might get rather repetitive. So just have in your mind that most of the tools can be employed for seizing opportunities as well as solving business issues. In fact, in many cases solving the issue *creates* the opportunity.

How to use this book

The Creative Problem Solver is divided into three parts. Personally I'd suggest that you read the whole thing, lightly and without any great effort, then when you're ready, go back to Part II, *Innovation*, and use it as needed during your problem-solving/opportunity-seizing sessions.

Overall, the idea is that while your problems might be difficult, the tools to solve them needn't be. You want to be able to get going as quickly and easily as possible: this book is set up for you to do just that.

Part I gives an insight into problem solving. The way our brains work, finding patterns, relying on past experiences, getting 'stuck in a rut' and how that can hold us back. It sets the scene for what follows.

Part II is the heart of the book. The 12 tools you need to meet big business challenges head on and seize upon your greatest opportunities. Each tool is simply explained, step-by-step, showcased with a business example and highlighted with a visual aid to use in your sessions.

And each tool has been written to be intuitive and energising, not process-heavy and wearying. As Elon Musk, billionaire co-founder of Tesla Motors and PayPal, says: 'I don't believe in process. The problem is that at a lot of big companies, process becomes a substitute for thinking. You're encouraged to behave like a little gear in a complex machine.'

Part III explores how to run a brainstorming session successfully.

At times you may be working alone – and these tools will help with your solo sessions. But you'll probably be doing much of the work as part of a team. And that will probably include a brainstorm of some kind (or 'mind shower', as some people call them for reasons I don't quite understand). Often I'll use the term 'session' to describe your group ideation (mainly because I hate the word ideation). But sometimes I'll say 'brainstorm', just because – while we all know traditional brainstorming can be flawed – it's an accepted term that doesn't look likely to go away anytime soon.

Anyway, in Part III we'll look at how to run those sessions successfully – we'll investigate what 'good brainstorming' looks like.

That will also include the background work you might want to do, how to get everyone working together, even how to use a flipchart (you'd be amazed how often potentially great brainstorm sessions are rendered useless by poor flipchart discipline).

We'll also look at how to take the great solutions you've come up with and help ensure they get off the flipchart, into the boardroom and then into the real world.

More at www.thinking-tools.co.uk

The pages of this book are 216 x 138mm. Which means you'll have to press the enlarge button a fair few times if you want to photocopy the visuals that accompany each thinking tool for your brainstorming sessions.

Alternatively there's a microsite at www.thinking-tools.co.uk. It has all of the visuals (each with a description) and a couple of other useful printouts so it's easier to get them the size you need to stick up somewhere prominent in your sessions. They also have white backgrounds to save on toner.

PART I
INSIGHT

'If you only have a hammer, you see every problem as a nail.' ABRAHAM MASLOW

I was catching a train, so I parked in the station car park I'd used a hundred times before. I called the pay by phone service . . . to discover it wasn't working. Luckily, my ashtray had enough change to feed the meter. As I got to the meter, another man was standing there, typing the phone number written on the meter into his smartphone. He'd just had a conversation with someone walking away, who I think had told him it wasn't working.

'The pay by phone isn't working,' I also told him. 'It's not recognising the location number.'

'I haven't got any choice,' he replied grumpily. 'I don't have enough change.'

It's stayed with me, that very brief conversation with a stranger. He knew the phone option wasn't working. But he didn't have enough change to pay by cash. So he 'had' to use the phone option . . . even though he knew it wasn't working. I found it quite unnerving, his bizarre bloody-mindedness. *I have the resources for Option A, but it doesn't work. Option B is working, but I don't have the resources for it. Err . . . Go back to Option A.*

Afterwards, I realised his reaction wasn't unique. In business, it's a mindset you might have come across before. 'Option A isn't working, but we don't have the resources to try Option B. So . . . let's stick with Option A.'

It's crazy, of course it is. What we should be doing is brainstorming how to get the resources for Option B. Or how to fix Option A. Or – and this can be the interesting bit – what Options C, D, E, F, G and H might be. But to do that we need to fix our thinking and stop being so narrow-minded and process driven.

As I mentioned in the introduction, I have a degree in psychology – but I'm no psychologist. Or neuroscientist. Or brain surgeon (clearly). So if you really want to know more about the way our brains work then I'd heartily recommend *Thinking, Fast and Slow* by Daniel Kahneman, *Emotional Intelligence* by Daniel Goleman and *The Tell-Tale Brain* by V. S. Ramachandran.

I can also recommend *Decoded* by Phil Barden, *The Decisive Moment* by Jonah Lehrer and *Incognito* by David Eagleman. All utterly compelling and convincing insights into how our brains work without lots of dreary talk of axons and dendrites. (Full details of these works and of other recommended reading are given at the end of the book.)

But here we're just interested in getting a little background into how the brain solves problems – so that we can play to its strengths and be aware of its weaknesses. Doing so also gives us some context as to why certain corporate approaches to problem solving can be pretty ineffectual.

Of course, if you're not fussed about the theory of why creative thinking tools work and you just want to get straight to using them, then please skip ahead to Part II, *Innovation* (it starts on page 13).

But just before you do, let me ask if you've ever tried this childish trick.

Ask someone what 's, i, l, k' spells. Then ask them to say 'silk' three times. Then ask them what cows drink. Most people will quickly say 'milk'. At which point, after a dramatic pause, you point out that no, cows drink water.

See how easy it is to fool our brains? Perhaps you'd better read on.

Where your brain is going wrong

'Life is tough, but it's tougher when you're stupid.' JOHN WAYNE

In 1997 a computer called Deep Blue beat world champion Garry Kasparov at chess.

Actually, let me clarify what happened. Garry Kasparov won their match in 1996, then (very narrowly) lost the rematch in 1997 against a Deep Blue which was aided by a group of IBM programmers and chess experts who directed and reprogrammed the computer between games. (They probably felt the need to reprogramme it after Kasparov won the opening battle in 45 moves.)

At the time, Deep Blue's victory was hailed as an incredible achievement in 'computer intelligence'. But I've always thought it was testament to just how amazing the human brain is. The computer had a team of programmers and chess experts behind it. Infinite memory. Phenomenal processing power. It couldn't be distracted. Wouldn't get emotional. And it never got tired. Yet it only just won the rematch.

And the reason Deep Blue struggled was that it took on the 86 billion neurons of an exceptional brain which its owner had spent most of his life training to do just one thing: win chess games.

And it's not just chess – footballers' brains are pretty impressive too. Honestly. Just think about a free kick. The player has to deal with the position of the ball on the pitch relative to the goal. The position of all the other players – where they currently are and where they might move to. Who those players are, what their individual strengths and weaknesses are. The wind strength and direction. How humid it is. Whether or not it's raining – and if so, how hard. The temperature. The physics of the ball moving in the air, which will vary according to how hard they hit it, where they hit it, in what way they hit it.

Plus their own level of energy and heart rate, which will change throughout the game. Do you know how difficult all that is? How incredibly complicated all those maths problems are? People use the term 'muscle memory', but that's doing the brain a disservice. And put it this way: there's currently no computer on Earth with the ability to take a free kick as well as a world-class footballer.

From science to arts to sport, from commerce to creativity, the human brain is tremendous at problem solving. Which is just as well, since it's what you're going to be using to solve whatever challenge your business is facing.

In fact, your brain is solving fiendishly-difficult problems all the time. It's just too modest to let your consciousness know. Here's another one that computers struggle with: recognising a chair and sitting on it. *You* can recognise a chair at a hundred paces; even one you've never seen before, painted a colour you've never seen a chair in before, and despite the fact that most of it is obscured by a coat that's been thrown on it. To a computer, recognising a chair is a tricky old task. To your brain, it's a mere trifle.

So what's the brain doing when it's solving problems? How does it come up with its answer?

PROBLEM-SOLVING TIP

Here's a very simple explanation of problem solving from an old *New Scientist* article by Helen Phillips ('FAQ: The Human Brain', September 2006): 'Solving problems can happen in two ways. It can be a type of thought or calculation – pulling information from memory, filtering new information, combining it all and weighing up alternatives. Or it can be a gut instinct – a decision made by the more primitive, emotional part of our brain, like the mental equivalent of a reflex. The most creative problem solving can be a long term process of both mulling things over in thought and in our unconscious mind, with the answer finally popping out.'

For one thing, our brain is taking in information every moment of every second of every day. And all that input comes through our five senses. In business, it's likely to be visual or aural input. Only during a business lunch does oral input become involved.

Then it processes that information. Input causes neurons to fire, to communicate with each other through synapses using an electrochemical process we don't need to understand (fortunately).

And, of course, it interprets that information. This is an important point – we don't all see the same input and come up with the same conclusion. Your past experiences, memories, personality, current mood and brain development will all affect how you interpret the stimuli pouring in through your senses.

And both your conscious and unconscious brain are involved. By definition, you're only aware of the conscious part. But that can often be comparatively serene – the swan gliding across the mill pond – while underneath your unconscious is pedalling furiously.

The unconscious genius

Neuroscientist David Cresswell ran an interesting study on the conscious versus unconscious in problem solving (in research findings presented at the 2012 NeuroLeadership Summit).

He asked people to think about buying an imaginary car, giving them a list of wants and needs to consider. One group had to choose immediately – and did pretty badly at making the optimal decision. A second group had more time to try to consciously solve the problem . . . yet their choices weren't much better.

But the third group . . . they were given the problem, then given a task to distract them – something that (lightly) held their conscious attention for a few minutes but allowed their unconscious to keep working. And this group did significantly better than the other two groups at selecting the best car overall.

Isn't that fascinating? When the conscious mind was distracted by an irrelevant activity, its decision-making skills actually got better. Which means we may be able to add *minor distractions* to a *change of scene*, a *complete break* and *humour* as environmental ways of helping our brains crack tricky tasks.

Here's another great example of the conscious and unconscious mind interacting, in a fairly well-known experiment by psychologists:

You're in a room with two cords hanging from the ceiling. The problem is, how can you tie the cords together when there's only you and the cords are too far apart to be grabbed at the same time?

A few people solve it without any help, by tying something small but heavy (their bunch of keys, perhaps) to one cord and swinging it like a pendulum so they can catch it while gripping the other cord.

Sometimes when people couldn't work it out, the researchers gave hints by 'accidentally' bumping into one cord so it swung slightly, after which more people cracked the problem. Yet when asked afterwards, many of them had no recollection of the hint. Once again, people's unconscious mind had got to work without them consciously realising.

I spot a pattern

The question is, how are our brains making these clever problem-solving leaps? Again and again, it's by finding (incredibly sophisticated) connections between different elements, and by pattern matching.

Like with the chair example from earlier: your brain is clever enough to recognise the pattern of a chair with a level of sophistication far beyond what a computer can manage. And as I say, your brain is too modest to even tell you that recognising a chair is a problem – it just gets on with the business of pointing out where it is so you can rest your weary legs.

Unconscious stupidity

OK, we're agreed: our brains are amazing. No wonder they're the most complex thing we've ever discovered.

But they're not perfect. Sometimes we might not want our unconscious brain to make connections or pattern-match, but it goes ahead anyway. It refuses to stop. Like with optical illusions: thanks to the wonder of rulers we know the two lines are the same length. But when one has arrowhead lines pointing inwards and the other has the same arrowhead lines swapped over so they point outwards, the former looks shorter than the latter. We just can't overrule the way our brains work, even though we know the answer it's coming up with is wrong.

There's a saying along the lines of, 'It's the height of stupidity to keep doing the same thing yet expect a different result', but that's what our unconscious minds do. And it's one reason why we need creative thinking tools – to force our brains to make new, unexpected connections and break out of their expected pattern matching.

Conscious stupidity

So, our unconscious brain has its shortcomings. But what about our conscious brain? We're aware of our conscious thinking, so surely that's easier to control? You'd think so, but sadly our conscious brain can be a bit thick too. Here are three examples of how and why.

i. We're not rational

Why do we overeat, particularly sugar and fat? Because we crave them. Why? Because sugar and fat are useful, high-calorie foods that in evolutionary terms were hard to come by. So we evolved so that our brains' opioids and dopamine react to foods with sugar and fat in them. In other words, they taste good. Really good. Because 200,000 years ago it meant we were prepared to put in the work needed to get these scarce resources.

Except: what happens when one person invents the corner shop and another invents the Mars bar? Suddenly high-calorie, high-fat, high-sugar foods are *not* hard to come by. But thanks to evolution they still taste really good. So we eat far more sugar and fat than is good for us. Even when doctors and scientists and meddlesome governments tell us they're not good for us.

Our brains know we don't need the Mars bar. Our brains know we might be better off skipping today's Mars bar. But we're not automatons, working logically, rationally and optimally. We're much more swayed by our emotions than we like to admit – and sometimes we even let our tongue do our brain's thinking. So not only do we still have the Mars bar, we grab a packet of Walker's crisps too.

ii. We're lazy

I mentioned Daniel Kahneman's brilliant book *Thinking, Fast and Slow* near the start of this *Insight* part and I can't recommend it enough. In it he relates an experiment you can try with colleagues:

> We've picked a man from the UK at random. His neighbours describe him as shy, withdrawn, polite and helpful – but not very interested in the real world. Now, is he more likely to be a farmer or a librarian?

Well, what do you think?

Most people say 'librarian' without hesitation.

In other words, they make a judgement based just on the information they were given. Or at least, the bulk of the information. Because there's one crucial point (the only absolute fact in the statement): 'We've picked a man from the UK at random.'

If you think about just that one fact, you'd say 'farmer'. Because of course there are many thousand more farms in the UK than there are libraries. And many of those farms will have more than one male farmer, whereas fewer libraries will have several male librarians.

Simple statistics show it's far more likely that he's a 'shy, withdrawn, polite farmer' than that he is a librarian. And you knew that, if you'd only bothered to think about it. But you don't – instead of thinking about the bigger picture, you just go on the information you're given at that moment. Your conscious brain was lazy and didn't bother to ask pertinent questions. Kahneman calls it 'WYSIATI' – What You See Is All There Is.

It's another shortcoming to be aware of in our problem solving – the assumption that the information we have to hand is all the information we need. And the assumption that there's nothing to gain by challenging what the information tells us.

iii. We like taking shortcuts

People often buy wine – and moisturiser – on the basis of price. Basically they think, 'What's the most I'm willing to spend on wine/moisturiser at this given moment?'

Because they assume that the more a bottle of wine costs, the better it will taste. And that the pricier a jar of moisturiser, the more expensive and efficacious its ingredients. Yet both assumptions have been proven to be unfounded.

So why do we do it? Because life's complicated enough without having to have memorised an Oz Clark book on vino before you pop to the off-licence, or have studied for a degree in beautology before you nip into Boots. We need a shortcut so we can avoid all that tedious, tiring thinking. And buying on price seems like a reasonable shortcut. Although, as I'm sure you know, in blind taste tests, putting the wine in order from favourite to least favourite *never* correlates with the order of price from most expensive to cheapest.

Traditional problem solving

The fleeting, top-line look at the brain we've just raced through is (probably) not enough for you to be able to roll up your sleeves, pick up a scalpel and perform a stereotactic brain biopsy. But it's enough to give us an idea of what the hero of our brainstorming sessions is like. We know a little of its strengths and weaknesses in problem solving.

Plus, we may have gained a little understanding into why traditional problem-solving approaches aren't giving us the breakthroughs we need.

Process prevents progress

Talk to people about what holds them back at work and there's one subject that crops up again and again. Process. Process. Process. Process prevents progress.

Yet paradoxically, many problem-solving approaches are, shall we say, 'process rich'.

And that's because we can (for the sake of simplicity) divide problem solving (or opportunity seizing) into two areas: analysis and insight. Both are usually important to be successful, and when you use the 12 creative thinking tools in *Innovation* you'll find that some have a more analytical lead, some more of an insight lead.

Many problem-solving structures focus too much on the process-heavy analytical approach, as if every problem is a jigsaw which just needs the pieces putting in the right order. Whereas many problems are more like jigsaws with several pieces missing. And all the analysis in the world isn't going to magic up those missing pieces.

Just do a quick 'problem solving' search online and you'll be deluged with flowcharts, process diagrams, layered pie charts, tables and complex schematics. Usually with a liberal sprinkling of arrows pointing from one box to another.

Here's a typical problem-solving structure I've dug up. It says that problem solving is a process of six steps:

1. Identify the problem

2. Structure the problem

3. Look for possible solutions

4. Make a decision

5. Implement

6. Monitor/seek feedback

The actual generation of ideas is just one of six steps. It gets no more prominence or contemplation than any of the others. And it's called 'Look for possible solutions', which gives you a clue as to how insipid its suggestions are. In fact, read through as many problem-solving strategies as I have and you sometimes get the impression that their creators are shying away from the crunch moment where they actually tell you *how* to come up with that spark of innovation.

What's obvious is that a purely analytical approach won't be enough. Following a process is rarely going to give you the spark that lights up the room (or people's faces).

What you need – to get your conscious and unconscious brain generating solutions and innovations like never before – is a creative thinking tool.

Or better yet, 12 of them.

PART II
INNOVATION

'If at first the idea is not absurd, there is no hope for it.' ALBERT EINSTEIN

i. Think bigger

ii. Think like another

iii. Be contrary

iv. Be constrained

v. Choice architecture

vi. Old + old = new

vii. Reverse engineering

viii. Sidestep the issue

ix. Random insertion

x. Interrogate and extrapolate

xi. Solve something simpler

xii. Combine and redefine

So here we are: 12 creative thinking tools to take your business further. To solve problems, seize on opportunities and innovate. This is the section you'll want to refer back to when you're running your sessions, for a refresher of the approaches and for choosing which ones to use when. I would always recommend that you use three or four approaches each time, to have the best chance of getting the best answer.

Each creative thinking tool is divided into five sections: *Visual, Theory, Action, Example* and *Summary.*

Visual

A simple visual aid to help you illustrate to others how the tool works. These are also available online at www.thinking-tools.co.uk to print out if you want to display them during your sessions.

Theory

Each tool starts with a brief explanation of *why* it works. Each will change the way you think about the issue or the way you interact with your environment (whether that's your colleagues, your processes or the way you conduct problem-solving sessions).

Action

Here's how to run the creative thinking tool during your brainstorming session.

The toolkit at the start (and subsequent explanation) will give a clear step-by-step guide, but each tool is described as simply as possible, focusing on the approach and mindset more than a minute-by-minute breakdown of the process. The tool will provide the 1 per cent inspiration. You (and your team) need to put in the 99 per cent perspiration.

Problem, opportunity or innovation?

There's a flipside to each of the tools too: they're often also great for opportunity-seizing. In fact, many of the world's most creative and innovative companies use these kinds of approaches for their most successful developments.

Look at Apple. Steve Jobs famously said, 'We don't do market research.' The world's most valuable company, committing multi-millions to product launches with integrated ecosystems and vast advertising campaigns . . . without any market research.

Why? Well for one thing, Apple wants to surprise and delight its customers. If you ask someone what they want for their birthday, they're hardly likely to be surprised when that's exactly what you give them.

But if you're not going to ask your customers what to do, and you want something bigger than an iterative step-change based on what you're already doing . . . then how are you going to make the breakthrough?

With many of the same creative thinking tools revealed here. And by exploring each tool you'll quickly discover how to flex it according to the use you're putting it to.

One more thing. For simplicity, the *action* describes the tool as if you're having a group brainstorm and you're going to spend 30–60 minutes using one tool to crack your problem.

That may not be the case, of course – and certainly, some of the approaches require longer to work through or may need you to do some advance prep. Take the time you need and don't expect that you'll necessarily solve your biggest business issues in one meeting you've got scheduled for a rainy Thursday afternoon. You may also be working alone rather than in a group, and that's fine too – there's more about brainstorming in Part III: *Inspiration.*

Example

Each tool has a case study to illustrate the principle – a demonstration of the sort of solution/breakthrough (and business success) that can be achieved using that specific approach. You might want to tell these stories to your colleagues when introducing the creative thinking approach, for inspiration.

Summary

I'll mention what kind of problem/opportunity that specific tool can be especially suited to, retread some of the key points and give a few pertinent questions you can ask when using the tool to ensure you're getting the most from it.

i.
Think bigger

'If a problem cannot be solved, enlarge it.'
Dwight D. Eisenhower

Let's start with a creative thinking tool that's very simple but also extremely powerful.

In a nutshell, it's this: take the problem you've been given, phrase it as a question, then step back to ask a bigger, broader question. It works because narrow, tightly defined problems can severely restrict the scope for a solution (and reduce the size of the achievement).

Broader problems allow for broader solutions – which can, surprisingly, be easier to solve. Simply because there are usually many more ways to solve them.

Visual

The smallest shape at the centre is your current problem. Each dot is an 'anchor' – a detail of the problem that defines its small, tight shape. As you think bigger, making the problem broader and more general, you start to lose these anchors. The problem becomes bigger, broader – and simpler.

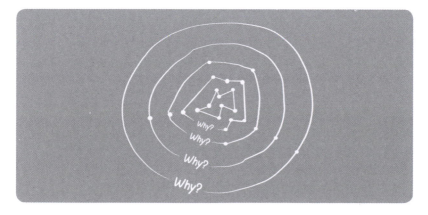

Theory

Our conscious mind is incredibly influenced by what's happening at that very moment. It's like those times when you're in a meeting, concentrating fully, and someone says, 'Not long 'til lunch'. Suddenly you start feeling hungry and that tray of sandwich triangles and mini samosas is all you can think about.

It's the same with problem solving. You're given a problem and your brain immediately starts trying to tackle the problem in the way it's been framed to you. It's what we're trained to do: deal with what we're given at that moment as quickly as possible.

But. You could stop. Step back. And instead of tackling the problem, tackle *the way the problem is expressed*. If the problem is represented by a circle, you're drawing a bigger circle around it and expressing what *that* problem is.

Why would you want to do such a thing – make the problem *bigger*? Well, often problems are difficult to solve because they are so tightly-defined that there really is no possible answer within their confines.

The theory is, by defining a bigger, broader problem you'll create more freedom around the way you can solve it. The more general the issue, the more possible solutions there are to it.

And instead of directly solving the initial problem, you're solving a bigger one that either solves the initial one as well, or renders it irrelevant.

Action

> **THINK BIGGER TOOLKIT**
>
> 1. Write out the problem as it stands, typically in the form of a question you want answered.
>
> 2. Then ask, 'What's the bigger issue behind that?' or 'Why is that an issue – what's the bigger picture of what we want to achieve?' to move to a broader level.
>
> 3. Keep asking 'why' and stepping back until you get to something truly transformative: a broader, more general iteration.
>
> 4. Now look at ways to answer that question – and the smaller one you started with will be solved too.

The first thing to do is avoid the temptation to try to solve the problem. Phrase it as a question, but ask people to steer away from solutions.

Instead, talk about *why* it's an issue – what's the *real* challenge/ ambition behind it? What's the bigger problem (or opportunity)? Why will solving that problem be a good thing – what achievement will it bring about?

Keep asking 'Why?' to step back to a bigger, broader level. Keep going until you get to a question that gives you the shivers: one you'd really like to answer to make a bigger business breakthrough.

> **PROBLEM-SOLVING TIP**
>
> A useful starting point can be to look at the *benefit* you'd get from solving the initial problem. You could then just ask, 'What would be a great way to achieve that benefit as massively as possible?' – and suddenly you've jumped to a broader level, a step back from the original, narrowly defined problem.

For instance, if your initial problem is, 'How do we make our battery 20 per cent lighter?' then let's ask:

'*Why* do we want to make the battery 20 per cent lighter?' The answer: 'Because then we'll save enough weight to be able to add a radio.'

OK, keep going: '*Why* do we want to add a radio?' 'Because the competition has introduced one to their product.'

Now we've moved up two levels in the space of two simple questions. The problem we've got to now is that the competition has added a radio to their product. And now we can ask a broader question, and find many more ways to answer it.

In the case of, 'How do we tackle the fact that the competition has introduced a radio?' it's clear that there are many more ways to solve that than there are, 'How do we make our battery 20 per cent lighter?'.

One answer to the competition problem is to add your own radio, and one way to be able to do that is make the battery lighter. But there may be other ways to add one too. Or there may be an alternative where you don't add a radio at all, you find a completely different way to counter your competitor. Maybe you just point out that radios in that product don't make sense, because they drain the battery faster, making the product less effective for its main function. Or maybe you have a radio and a heavier product, but you focus on how rugged and sturdy yours is, compared to the lightweight, 'flimsy' competition.

Or, maybe you add a different (lighter) feature that's superior to having a radio. Making the product waterproof, perhaps, as Sony did with its Xperia smartphones. Brainstorm new features and you might have something interesting, innovative and differentiating, rather than playing at being a *me-too* catch-up.

The power of 'why'

I'm sure you get the point. It's easy to lose sight of the wood for the trees. You get a narrow problem and you start solving it narrowly, forgetting to 'question the question', step back and ask 'Why?' to think more broadly and generally about what it is really you want to achieve.

Here's another 'for instance'. If you run an airline and customers are telling you, 'I hate flying long-haul, the time it takes to get from A to B is really tedious and frustrating', you might think the problem is, 'We need to make long-haul flights quicker'. You might create a fleet of Concordes or some such, at phenomenal expense and fuel consumption.

But that's because you're solving the problem in the way it's been couched. You're limiting the scope of your solution to the way the customers have phrased the problem. But think back to Steve Jobs: 'We don't do market research.' He recognised that customers didn't always know what they want. Same here: they don't necessarily know what the problem is.

They're bored and frustrated, so they're suggesting the flight time is too long. So you're trying to make it shorter. But what if you *think bigger*? What if instead of asking 'How can we reduce our flight time to stop our customers becoming bored and frustrated?' you just ask the broader, second part of that question, 'How can we stop our customers becoming bored?'

And so airlines invent in-flight movies and games. They break up the flight time with welcome drinks, then the meal, then the snacks. The captain keeps you updated on where you are above the Earth. Now, some airlines are starting to offer WiFi. And the cabin crew do their best to look after you and make sure you've got everything you need.

Take this to the extreme, and – for less than the price of a fleet of Concordes – you could create a flight experience so enjoyable (with the latest movies, free bar, massage chairs and supermodels for cabin staff) that people actually want the flight time to be *longer*, not shorter.

So solve the bigger issue for three good reasons:

1. It can be easier, because your thinking can be bigger too – you've got more room for manoeuvre.

2. It means the original problem is negated, so no longer matters.

3. It often gives you a solution that achieves more than solving the original problem would have done.

> **PROBLEM-SOLVING TIP**
>
> At Toyota, they have something they call the 'Five Why Process'. When a problem occurs, they ask *Why* it happened. Then *Why* again and again (yes, five times in all) to ensure they're really getting to the root cause. Then they solve *that*.

Think bigger is also useful when you're looking at maximising an opportunity, not just solving a problem. To return to airlines for a moment, once upon a time British Airways was going to run with the strapline, 'The world's biggest airline'. It was literal. It was dull. And it was difficult to use as the focus of an engaging marketing campaign – it's all 'head' and no 'heart'.

So they thought broader.

They took the key word 'biggest', meaning literally having the most customers, and they thought about broader descriptions. And came up with 'The world's *favourite* airline'.

Sounds very simple – and it is – but that simple change became a very memorable, emotive strapline. It gave them a warmer, friendlier positioning and the opportunity to create much more iconic advertising that had emotion rather than just a sense of scale.

Example

One of the clients I've worked with for many years is Halifax. They are absolutely committed to being a 'challenger brand' (a term coined by Adam Morgan in his book *Eating the Big Fish*). Which means they're always looking for ways to do things a little differently to other banks.

One of the many financial services they offer is savings accounts. And I was once in a problem-solving workshop where marketers in the Halifax savings team were discussing a speed-to-market issue.

The problem was this: they felt that as a bank, they were slower than many of their competitors at updating their advertising and marketing literature. So if a competitor changed its savings rate (say, improved it by 0.25 per cent AER), Halifax would change its rates too, but seemingly be slower than other banks to publicise the fact. So Halifax would, during that update delay, seem to be offering an uncompetitive savings rate compared to other banks.

Resulting in savers leaving them for the competition.

So their problem was a simple one: How can we increase our speed to market?

It's a perfectly reasonable problem to arrive at and it's also perfectly solvable with many of the tools in this book.

But let's take a step back. And answer a bigger, broader challenge.

First of all, *why*?

Why do they want to increase their speed to market? Because being slow is losing them market share. Savers don't want to join them or stay with them because their savings rate seems uncompetitive.

So now it's easy to ask a bigger question: 'How can we attract and keep savers?'

In fact, let's be really bold and say, 'How can we attract and keep savers without offering the highest savings rate?' Because if you can answer that problem, the original problem will never occur again.

Giving yourself some freedom

It's obviously a much bigger question to answer, but it has a clear advantage over the 'speed to market' problem they'd set themselves.

Because now we're looking for *any* way to incentivise savers to join (apart from just offering the best rate), which gives us lots of freedom compared to the narrow range of possibilities that might be available for the 'speed up the literature production process' problem.

So, what could Halifax do to attract and keep savers without offering the highest savings rates?

Clearly, if the savings rate isn't going to be the best on the market, they needed to start offering something *in addition* to the rate.

It could have been a service-led proposition, but Halifax isn't about service and relationships, it's about great value. Plus, if as a bank you're not going to worry about having the best interest rate, you might want to start by looking at how you could incentivise customers financially in some other way.

Now, this issue arose at a time when the Bank of England interest rate was at a record low. So savings rates everywhere were very low anyway. In fact my IFA suggested I put my savings into Premium Bonds. I wouldn't lose any money, I could take it out whenever I wanted . . . but I had the chance of winning a big lump sum too.

Because that was the choice you had: put your cash into a savings account where you'd get a very low rate of interest, or put it into Premium Bonds where you might win big, but you'd get no interest at all so your money could still lose value over time.

Halifax simply brought these two benefits together. They invented the *Savers Prize Draw*. An instant access savings account that paid annual interest. But which automatically entered you into a prize draw to win one of three prizes of £100,000 every single month, provided your balance was over a certain amount.

Eureka! Now you've got a traditional savings account that customers understand and are comfortable with. But with a unique reason to stay: the chance to win money like Premium Bonds.

And suddenly, it doesn't matter if your competitor offers 0.25 per cent more interest than you do. No one's going to leave you for an extra six quid in interest per year if it means losing out on the chance to win £100,000 every month. So you don't need to get into a panic changing your rates as quickly as possible (and saving you the cost of having to change your literature each time too).

A brilliant solution. All achieved by taking the original problem, expressed as a question, and stepping back to something bigger and broader. By challenging the assumption that responding faster to competitors' rate changes was the need. And by recognising that incentivising customers to join and stay was the real issue, and then freely exploring new, bigger, bolder ways to achieve that.

Summary

Think bigger is about broadening your horizons. Breaking out of the little bubble you've found yourself in and moving to ever increasing circles of influence.

It's equally as useful for innovating as it is for problem solving. In fact, solving a problem with this tool can often lead *to* an innovation.

It's well suited to problems to do with business processes (as in the Halifax example above). And it's also useful when you suspect the problem is a result of 'silo mentality' – teams or departments working in isolation without looking at the business as a whole. After all, by thinking bigger, it's inevitable that the change will be bigger, involve more people and generate results that are more sweeping and far-reaching.

Again, like with the Halifax example, the people faced with (and responsible for) the problem of their advertising and marketing literature processes being slow could have 'just' found ways to speed the process up, and gone ahead by themselves. But coming up with a breakthrough like the Savers Prize Draw was a much bigger undertaking – one that they couldn't execute without getting many more departments involved and really energising the whole company.

Finally, to use *think bigger* successfully, ask:

- Have we got so caught up in our day-to-day challenges that we've lost sight of the bigger picture?

- What is our business – our whole business – about? If we remind ourselves of that, and look at our problem in that context, can we *think bigger*?

- What's the broader issue behind our specific problem?

- Why do we want to solve this problem? Why do we want to achieve that benefit? OK, and why do we want to achieve that? Why? Why?

- What advantage would solving the problem give us? What are other ways to achieve that?
- Are we prepared to put in the hard yards to get everyone who needs to be involved with our big idea on board?

ii.
Think like another

'Again and again, the impossible problem is solved when we see that the problem is only a tough decision waiting to be made.' ROBERT H. SCHULLER

There are three versions of this tool here; each is a great way of getting individuals and groups thinking a little differently, by asking them to think like someone (or something) else.

Visual

Think of another brand or famous person you could become, for instance:

Stephen Fry, Boris Johnson, Anna Wintour, Jeremy Clarkson, Batman, Shakespeare, Gandalf, David Bowie, Sharon Osbourne, Bradley Wiggins, The Dalai Lama, Kim Kardashian . . .

Virgin, First Direct, Apple, Primark, Innocent, Coke, 3M, M&S, McDonalds . . .

They have different qualities from you (and each other), so they'd approach the problem in a different way. Look at how the chart plots six people on a scale of analytical approach and people approach, for instance. Ignore where they're actually plotted – it's not supposed to be an accurate portrayal of their personalities.

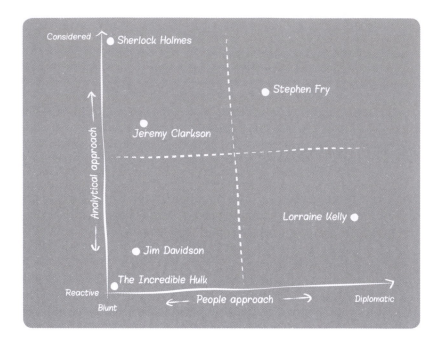

Theory

I went to a murder mystery dinner party a couple of years ago. You might know them: every guest plays a different character and there's a CD that gives little snippets of plot while the guests get tasks to do during the meal and lines of dialogue to deliver. All while trying to work out who the murderer is and why.

When people role play like that, they're often able to conjure up a very different personality from their usual one. Shy people, for instance, when dressed up to look different and forced to put on a comedy accent, can actually become surprisingly bold and outgoing. Incredibly nice, heart-of-gold types can transform themselves into chillingly Machiavellian baddies, capable of adding evil flourishes to the character they've been given.

OK, it's acting. But the point is, these aren't professional actors. Yet relatively easily, they're able to behave very differently when required. They start feeling different. And thinking differently.

Which, for problem solving or opportunity seizing, can be very useful. We all know that not everyone thinks the same way. So if you can think like someone else for a while, you'll come up with quite different thoughts . . . and different answers.

It's a mental trick, giving yourself permission to think more freely and shed the constraints and restrictions you normally carry around – just like the guests at a murder mystery dinner party.

PROBLEM-SOLVING TIP

Surprisingly, a study by Evan Polman and Kyle J. Emich found you're more likely to solve a difficult problem on someone else's behalf rather than for yourself ('Decisions for others are more creative than decisions for the self', *Personality and Social Psychology Bulletin* 37(4), 2011). 'A prisoner was attempting to escape from a tower. He found a rope in his cell that was half as long enough to permit him to reach the ground safely. He cut the rope in half, tied the two parts together, and escaped. How could he have done this?' 66 per cent of test subjects who imagined this stranger in the tower found the solution compared with just 48 per cent of people asked to imagine it was themselves in the tower. (You split the rope lengthwise, obviously.)

Action

THINK LIKE ANOTHER TOOLKIT

1. Stop being yourself. Forget that you work at company X, with such-and-such a brand/history/process/restriction.

2. Get into the mindset of someone or something else – a famous person, a brand or a child.

3. Try being that brand/person in a bit of role play, to 'walk in their shoes'.

4. Now go back to the problem/opportunity and role play solving it from that person or brand's perspective.

5. Free of your usual constraints, but with the sharp focus that thinking like someone else brings, you'll unearth new, previously unconsidered solutions.

To use this approach successfully, you need to start by deciding who or what you want to take the perspective of. There's really no restriction, but the more different from your own personality or your company's brand, the more likely you are to get a real shift in thinking.

The main three 'roles' I'd recommend are:

1. Think like another brand.

2. Think like another person (one the whole group knows, someone who is almost certainly successful in their field, often a celebrity).

3. Think like a child.

If you're working in a group it can be enjoyable (and enjoyment creates useful, positive energy in brainstorming sessions) for people to choose who they'd like to approach the problem as (alternatively there are some suggestions in the visual).

The next step is to discuss that brand's/person's nature and approach.

> **PROBLEM-SOLVING TIP**
>
> Put yourself in the shoes of the person/brand you're being like. What is it about them that you might admire? What three words describe them? What are the clearest, strongest things you can say about the way they do things? You don't have to get this 'right'; you're just using that person or brand as a springboard for 'thinking up a different way of thinking'.

Let's say you choose Amazon. There are lots of things you could say about the way Amazon do things, but one of the things they've really pushed is automation. They've used logistics and computers to do things in the most efficient way – for example, when a 'picker' collects items from the warehouse, their handheld device will show them the most efficient route to take to collect the things they need. So how could you solve your problem with that Amazon focus on efficiency, streamlined processes and automation? How could you remove people from the process? How could you rearrange/rebuild your processes to solve (or neutralise) the problem?

Or how about a brand that's more about personality: Ben & Jerry's, the ice cream.

Think about what they do: sell ice cream. Lots of companies do that. Lots of much bigger companies. So maybe their problem was: 'How do we stand out from the market?' In fact, 'How do we stand out and successfully charge a premium?'

In their case, by creating a distinctive and fun brand. By having crazy names for their flavours, admitting that the small-scale way they mixed their ingredients meant sometimes you'd get a few more chocolate chunks, sometimes a few less, and touring in a 'cowmobile' so people can taste new recipes. In lots of little ways they've made their product more interesting and unexpected, not simply about taste or price.

Can you solve your issue by approaching it with a 'Let's make it fun, let's do something deliberately quirky' attitude like them?

Be famous – real or fictitious, dead or alive

If you've done thinking like another brand, try a famous person – real or fictitious, alive or dead. How would Stephen Fry approach it? Boris Johnson? Anna Wintour? Jeremy Clarkson? Batman? Shakespeare? Gandalf? The Dalai Lama?

As I say, you don't have to get their personality right. It's not about accurate portrayals, it's about creating a shortcut to a different way of thinking. So, for instance, you might say:

Jeremy Clarkson: 'He's very macho, very decisive, doesn't care about ruffling feathers. So let's approach things like that – bulldozing our way through no matter who we offend.'

Lorraine Kelly: 'She always shows lots of empathy and finds fun ways of making the experience enjoyable for everyone involved. So let's look at the problem in that way.'

Batman: 'He's a superhero without any superpowers – instead he uses technology and clever inventions adapted from other sources to achieve his solutions. How could we take the technology from another area and adapt it to solve our issue/achieve our goal?'

You get the idea. Here's one more 'for instance': the Team GB cycling team. Their approach under Dave Brailsford has been 'the aggregation of marginal gains'. In other words, any tiny little thing that they think might make even the smallest incremental difference, they'll do. Because those details can add up to something big (in their case, a huge haul of gold medals at the Olympics). Things like finding a slightly more aerodynamic material for their clothing. A thinner paint. Or bringing their own pillows with them when they travel, so they sleep well and are better rested.

Again, perhaps that approach might work for your problem. Think like Dave Brailsford and instead of trying to solve your problem with one blow from a sledgehammer, give it a thousand tiny taps; every tiny little change or improvement you can think of to add up to the result you want.

To see what this approach looks like in action, on YouTube search for 'If Microsoft designed iPod packaging' and you'll find a video that wittily shows the difference between Apple's approach to designing a product box and Microsoft's.

Be childish

The third approach in *think like another* is not to think like a celebrity or brand or company or someone you admire, but simply to think like a child.

That takes a bit more role playing, such as getting out some children's books, maybe some crayons or poster paints, perhaps even watching a TV programme aimed at children under 10. But it really works: a study quoted by Jonah Lehrer in his book *Imagine* found that people who were asked to imagine they were a seven-year-old child solved problems more innovatively than those who weren't.

If you've got children you'll understand why that may be the case – they don't impose the same restrictions on their thinking the rest of us do. They make surprising connections, they are playful, they ask unaskable questions and they don't get self-conscious about what they're saying. They're also very imaginative. It seems strange (and rather a shame) that this sort of creativity actually seems to diminish as we get older. We normally think of our cognitive skills as increasing with adulthood, but this one seems to go the other way.

So think like a child. Use simple language. Don't let sophisticated arguments discourage you. Use coloured pens. Draw your ideas. Make crazy connections. Turn your problem into a cartoon baddie you're going to defeat. Act out the problem and improvise the solution (look at how children will improvise with whatever's at hand to achieve their goal). And have some innocent fun – you'll be surprised how effective embracing your inner child can be.

PROBLEM-SOLVING TIP

Thinking like a child can be effective in problem solving; asking an actual child may not be. An MRI study of brain development revealed that the brain's centre of problem solving is among the last to mature. It found that higher-order brain centres like the prefrontal cortex don't fully develop until young adulthood.

Example

This is an *opportunity-seizing* example, courtesy of Michael O'Leary and Ryanair. Mr O'Leary has helped grow Ryanair into one of Europe's most successful airlines, employing over 8,500 people and with annual revenues of over €3 billion.

But the way he's achieved that success has brought about tremendous criticism – both for the company and him personally. The very approach that he gets slated for – by customers, regulators, competitors and the press – is the same approach that has brought him enormous success. How?

It's very easy to summarise his approach because it was so single-minded. When you look at European airlines pre-O'Leary, you can see just how different flying was considered to be compared to any other form of travel. It was much more expensive, but it was also more indulgent. Airlines competed on the basis of great service, comfort and experience.

There was an expectation that even if you were looking for the cheapest budget flight you could find, there'd still be a reasonable level of comfort. You'd still get an allocated seat, for instance. You'd still be able to take on a decent luggage allowance. And of course there'd still be 'complimentary' food during the flight.

This was the opportunity O'Leary saw. Other airlines believed you had to offer customers a certain level of comfort and service – so even a supposedly 'budget' flight would still have to bear all of the costs of providing that comfort and service.

O'Leary believed there were plenty of people who didn't care about that stuff – or at least, didn't care enough about it to pay more than they had to. He believed that people would happily eschew all that for a cheaper price. Heck, maybe they'd even settle for landing at a minor airport that was a coach journey away from the main airport, if it meant they'd save a few quid.

Instead of thinking like the other airline bosses, he thought like the boss of a completely different company – a budget supermarket maybe. Or you could say he thought like Jack Monroe, the amazing 'austerity chef' – looking for every possible angle from which to do something as cheaply as possible.

So he said, 'We promise to get you from A to B at the lowest possible price. And that's *all* we'll promise.' So he did away with huge swathes of comfort and service. They either disappeared completely, or they became options you paid extra for.

Which means no allocated seats, no meal, no movies, the seats don't recline and there are no pockets on the back of seats (to make cleaning and therefore turnaround times quicker). He's also allegedly suggested charging heavier customers more, charging customers to use the toilets and asking passengers to carry their own checked-in luggage to the plane, to cut costs (and therefore prices) further.

And, as I say, it's worked tremendously well. That laser-sharp focus on 'how can we make the price lower – because that's the only thing that matters' has brought Ryanair huge success and great profits. Because Michael O'Leary didn't think the way other airline chiefs did.

'The only thing worse than being talked about is not being talked about'

It's also interesting to go back to the criticism O'Leary and Ryanair have received for their practices: the airline has had, it might be said, a fair few unhappy customers. And that would normally be a no-no: most companies would go out of their way to avoid unhappy, complaining, critical customers – especially in the social media age when people are straight onto TripAdvisor or Twitter or Facebook to publicise their displeasure.

In fact, O'Leary has said, 'Short of committing murder, negative publicity sells more seats than positive publicity. Negative publicity generates so much more free publicity that it sells more tickets.'

People may groan and grumble, but when they go online to book their flight . . . many choose the cheapest carrier they can find, so they've got more money for their actual holiday.

An example of phenomenal growth by someone who dared to *think like another*. And in fact Michael O'Leary is someone you can have on your list of people to try and think like, aping his approach of 'This one thing matters and absolutely nothing else. In fact, anything that hinders that one thing or reduces its potential has to go.'

In his case, that one thing was 'the lowest possible price'. For you, it can be whatever you want it to be.

Summary

Think like another is a useful tool for getting your group engaged; for that reason it can be one to try early on. Often it's fun role playing at being a celebrity or a favourite brand or a child, and it will get people enthused and interacting. It's also good for both problem solving and opportunity seizing.

And it's a useful tool when your group involves people who are, shall we say, 'set in their ways' and who always approach things in the same way. This tool gives them a 'safe' way to think differently, because for once they're *not* being themselves. They're not, in that moment, even being people who work at that company.

That also makes the tool effective when the brainstorming group involves people who you suspect might be part of the problem, due to their rigid thinking. Giving them 'permission' to not be themselves with their already-established view can work wonders.

Think like a child is particularly suited to problems where people are weighed down by complexity and intangibles and esoteric issues. Children don't bother with those things, so it sweeps them away at a stroke – often revealing that they were meaningless barriers, not real issues at all.

Finally, to use *think like another* successfully, ask:

- Is the mood of the group a little flat, and so likely to benefit from early use of *think like another*, one of the more 'fun' tools in our thinking kit?

- What brand or celebrity has a trait we think could be useful here?

- In discussion, what brand or celebrity seems to get the group fired up?

- Are we spending enough time using props and media to start feeling like another brand/celebrity or a child, so we're in a different frame of mind *before* we start tackling the problem/ opportunity?

- But are we remembering to focus on utilising the trait they have, rather than getting carried away trying to faithfully imitate that person?

iii.
Be contrary

'If we all worked on the assumption that what is accepted as true is really true, there would be little hope of advance.' ORVILLE WRIGHT

Assumptions. Habits. Conventions. Routines.

All anathema to new thinking.

We fall into patterns of doing – and thinking – and miss out on finding a better way. In other words, just because it ain't broke, doesn't mean you can't fix it anyway.

Because when it comes to solving a problem – or capitalising on an opportunity or developing an innovation – there'll be lots of assumptions everyone involved will make, and a great many conventions you'll observe. So let's challenge those conventions. Let's be deliberately contrary and say 'Why does it have to be done that way?'

It's like that idea of travelling to work a different way every day. You travel the same way each day and your brain turns off. Take a new route and you might notice something different which might get your brain thinking. By challenging the conventional route you take, who knows what magic could happen?

Visual

Challenge conventions and remove the barriers from your thinking and suddenly many more new possibilities are opened up.

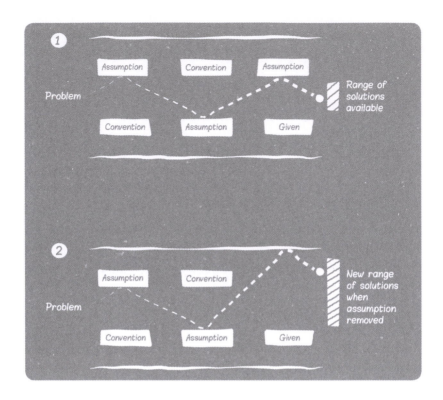

Theory

Be contrary is a direct response to some of the things we looked at in Part I to do with the way the brain works. To survive an absurdly complicated world, we create patterns and follow routines. If we had to consciously weigh up the pros and cons of every decision and consider every alternative – well, we'd be paralysed with indecision. And clinically insane.

So most of the time, conventions are useful. But not always when it comes to problem solving. For instance, in 2005 Microsoft released the Xbox 360 and in 2006 Sony released the Playstation 3. And what did they focus and compete on? Power. How many polygons they could draw at what frame rate. It had become the convention: a games console had to use the latest chips and have the maximum memory possible. And all the hype and marketing was around their specs. It's baffling to look back and recall how they really did use to talk about polygons.

And then . . . along came the Nintendo Wii. It didn't compete on power. It challenged the convention that 'faster is better'. It dared to be contrary, deliberately releasing a cheaper, more accessible console that was less powerful . . . but which focused on being fun, with imaginative games and innovative controls.

And as a strategy, being contrary worked. Microsoft sold around 77 million Xbox 360s. Sony around 75 million PS3s. While Nintendo has sold over 100 million Wiis – and apparently earns more profit on the sale of its console than either Microsoft or Sony do on their more expensive devices.

So the theory is that by looking at our assumptions and conventions and challenging them, we can free ourselves up to develop radically different answers. Reframe the problem by changing the way you allow yourself to tackle it.

You just have to pause and take a step back to question every element in turn – and you might be surprised how many assumptions are made on every project you're involved with.

Action

BE CONTRARY TOOLKIT

1. Before looking at the problem, look at the assumptions and conventions around the problem.

2. Now dare to be contrary – take the stance that it doesn't have to be like that; you could do things differently; you could ignore those conventions and start with a clean slate.

3. Notice how changing the rules of the game reframes the way the problem can be tackled – and frees you up to come up with exciting, groundbreaking new solutions.

If *think bigger* is, to some extent, about looking at the problem and saying, 'Why is that a problem?', then *be contrary* is about saying, 'Why does the problem have to be tackled like that? What would we do if we didn't have to do it that way?'

For instance, a car company has created a great new advertising campaign. But the legal and compliance department won't sign it off – they think it's ambiguous and could fall foul of the Advertising Standards Authority.

So the company has a problem to solve – amending the campaign to get through legal while still being great advertising.

PROBLEM-SOLVING TIP

Ignore logic. Our internal logic gets things wrong all the time – but we rarely challenge it. We make an instant appraisal and think, 'Oh, that's obvious, of course that's the case'. But amazing breakthroughs have been made by people who tried something that seemed to defy logic and confound the obvious.

A trivial example perhaps, but a supermarket was offering jam tasting to try to increase sales. They found that offering a choice of 24 jams got more people tasting them than when they just offered six. Seems obvious perhaps: more choice, more people interested. Yet interestingly … fewer sales. Logic would suggest that if you're getting more people trying the jam, you'll get more sales too. But actually, while they got fewer 'leads' (tasters) with just six jam choices, they got a much higher conversion rate (buyers). And more sales overall. So try ignoring what seems 'logical' and 'obvious' once in a while. You might be surprised by the results.

But wait: we've made an assumption straight away. That the advertising has to be signed off by the legal and compliance department. What if the business was contrary, and took the decision to ignore the legal beagles, and run the campaign as it stands? Sure, they might get into trouble. But maybe they wouldn't. And maybe if they did, the fine could be considered part of the marketing costs, if they thought the PR would be worth it.

See what I mean? We just make so many assumptions in business and follow an endless stream of conventions – and we rarely even realise it. This is the critical action you must take: with fresh eyes (and this is where involving people who are not close to the issue can help) identify the assumptions you've already made and the conventions you've already started observing just in the way you've framed the problem/opportunity.

Three simple starting steps

1. First ask if it's the conventions you're observing that are potentially the real problem (like with the car ad campaign above).

2. If not, look at whether or not *the problem itself* is a convention that could be tackled (like with the 'We need a really powerful console' challenge Nintendo were contrary with).

3. If you're still going, start to discuss the problem and how you might solve it – and as you do, make a note of the conventions you're following and assumptions you're making. Write those conventions out on the flipchart and you can go back as a group and *be contrary* with each of them in turn.

PROBLEM-SOLVING TIP

To get the most from this tool it's important not to say, 'Could we maybe possibly perhaps do this differently?' but to be contrary and say, 'We *will* do this differently'. Being contrary and challenging conventions is very powerful, but by its nature is going to get some people's backs up. You're going to need real determination to challenge the 'But that's the way we've always done it' mentality.

Keep saying, 'Why does it have to be like that? What would we do if it wasn't? What are we taking for granted about the problem? What are we ignoring because it's 'a given'?'

It's like a picture I saw once of people queuing at a government office somewhere in Asia. Except they weren't queuing: they were all sitting on the benches in the waiting room. So how did they know whose turn it was? Because they'd all taken their footwear off, and created a queue of shoes leading up to the counter. Because they'd challenged the 'given' of having to physically stand in line in order to still have an orderly queue.

At this point you'll have identified at least one convention; maybe several. Time to be contrary. Time to say: we're not going to follow that 'rule'. We're not going to say that's a 'given'. This is where you challenge what you can and can't do to solve the problem – because if you can break down some of those barriers, you can solve the problem more easily, or discover that you can just do something different (like Nintendo did) rather than solve the initial problem you began with.

The action may be to ignore all of the processes and procedures your company currently has. Because being contrary means daring to be different. It means removing obstacles.

This is particularly powerful – and important – if you're involved in a business with a legacy product/service/process. By legacy I simply mean, 'It's been around and fundamentally unchanged for a very long time'.

For instance, I had *Encyclopaedia Britannica* as a client at an agency I worked at – and their business was based on a legacy product: a huge stack of 32 physical encyclopaedias. They were very expensive to produce, and as sales fell they became cost prohibitive. And sales did indeed fall – spectacularly plummet, in fact – because they were from a bygone, pre-internet age, when people went to libraries and consulted reference books for information. And they just couldn't compete with Wikipedia for speed, convenience, breadth, depth or up-to-the-minuteness.

The company was a classic example of needing to challenge every convention about the way their business worked in order to compete. And every day they failed to do this, their business fell further behind.

Create the new normal

Be contrary may mean you look beyond the problem you've got to solve (or opportunity you want to seize) and spend time thinking about things which normally don't get any thought – the established practices that usually make life easier, but which may be getting in the way of a leap forward.

Example

The story I've heard involves a man called James, who had a love of chocolate. And who one day decided to start his own chocolate desserts company. He planned to call it *The Belgium Chocolate Company.*

There was a lot to sort out, naturally – including briefing an agency to come up with a brand for the business. So he appointed an agency (Big Fish) while he got to work on the recipes, product testing, sourcing ingredients, liaison with the supermarkets and so on.

After a few weeks, he realised he hadn't heard from the agency. So he gave them a call. 'Ah,' they said, 'the chocolate dessert brand. Hmm. You'd better come in.'

So James went to see them.

'It's not good news,' went the agency presentation. 'We were researching the market, and we discovered this has just launched.' And they showed him the packaging and advertising for Gü. 'Look at this luxurious, evocative brand,' they said. 'The chocolate and black packaging, the swirls, the language, the little black pots – even the name, fun yet appealing, with an umlaut over the 'u' like a smiley. If only you'd been a bit quicker – we think this is the sort of thing that could have worked for you. But they're a competitor.'

And James, seeing he'd been beaten to the punch, was furious. 'This . . . this is a disaster. I can't believe it! I can't believe they've done this before me! This is exactly the brand I should have!'

At which point the man from the agency paused. And looked James in the eye.

'Well,' he said, 'If that's how you really feel . . . then I've got some good news. Because this isn't a competitor that's just launched. It's the brand we've developed for you.'

James went ahead with Gü. And sold it six years later for £26 million.

> **PROBLEM-SOLVING TIP**
>
> Swatch is a good example of being contrary to solve a problem. They challenged the convention that Swiss watches needed to be serious, expensive timepieces focusing on heritage. Instead they introduced inexpensive fashion watches – rejuvenating the Swiss watch industry when it was being hammered by Japanese manufacturers like Seiko.

But what I love is the contrariness of the agency's presentation. The usual approach, of course, is to show the client the work you've done for them and explain why it's so great. Their simple twist on that convention was to show the client work which was apparently done by someone else for someone else, and explain why that was so great.

Instead of showing the client the work he could have, they showed him work which, apparently, he *couldn't* have. Which only made him want it more.

And it's a simple demonstration of how so many business conventions we take for granted can be turned on their head to do something new, unexpected and marvellous.

Summary

Be contrary is good for transformative solutions – like *think bigger*, it often yields far-reaching answers. So it's great when you want people to sit up and take notice – its unconventional, paradigm-shifting results will demand attention.

Whilst extremely simple, it can sometimes be challenging. First, people involved with the issue are often too close to it to realise they're making lots of assumptions.

And second, people sometimes struggle with breaking conventions. In many large organisations it's fair to say that while someone's career might suffer by taking a risk that doesn't come off, they're unlikely to experience the same setback by simply being utterly risk-averse all their working life – even though in many fields that's not going to take the business forward (and may see it fall behind the competition).

Finally, to use *be contrary* successfully, ask:

- What's the longest list we can compile of all the conventions we're following and assumptions we're making?

- Which of those would we find it helpful to remove, ignore, change or turn on its head?

- Is the problem a convention in itself? Can we be contrary and say 'The problem we thought we had . . . isn't the real problem, it's *this* instead'?

- Keep asking 'Why does it have to be done that way? What are we taking for granted? What's a "given" that actually we need to question?'

- Are we alert to any instances of suddenly following a convention during the session? If so, will we be sure to stop and challenge them?

iv.
Be constrained

'The more constraints one imposes, the more one frees oneself. And the arbitrariness of the constraint serves only to obtain precision of execution.' IGOR STRAVINSKY

Sometimes you can have too much freedom. Like a red setter let off the lead, your mind can go bounding off enthusiastically … but end up lost and panting.

And sometimes if you can do anything, you end up doing nothing.

But give yourself an artificial constraint – and by forcing your brain to think around this new, arbitrary obstacle, you may come up with an interesting new idea.

Alternatively, you can introduce a constraint that's not arbitrary but adds something desirable. It's different from having a problem that *has* to be solved, it's introducing a constraint that other companies aren't looking at (because it's not a problem they *need* to solve). By forcing yourself to introduce it, you create a great new opportunity.

Visual

Using a constraint is about narrowing the options, not so you (necessarily) get there quicker, but so you get somewhere different. In diagram 1 there's no constraint and you come up with solution A, same as everyone else. But in diagram 2, the constraint cuts off solution A and creates the chances of finding solutions B, C and D.

Some examples of constraints you can try are: the solution must cost nothing; must be implementable within a day; must be the first of its kind; must be popular; must be controversial; must remove an existing element; must not be technological; must not involve people; must make things simpler.

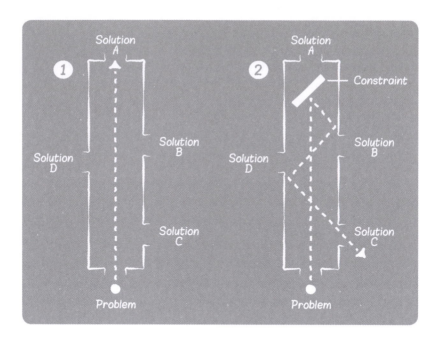

Theory

When I was at university I played the drums in a student rock band. After one particular gig at a hall of residence, we were sitting in the bar having a drink and recovering from our exertions. Especially me – I'd been banging hell out of my drumkit, spinning the drumsticks, throwing them in the air, barking backing vocals, giving it my all.

Along came a couple of girls: new fans! They asked the vocalist: 'Hi. Will you go back on stage and play a Red Hot Chili Peppers song?' The vocalist shook his head. 'Can't,' he said. 'We don't know any.' Undeterred, the girls turned to the lead guitarist: 'Oh go on, please, play a Chili Peppers song.' 'We can't,' said the guitarist, 'We just don't know any.' The girls pursed their lips and moved along the row of stools to the bassist. They implored him, too, to play a Chilis' song, and, again, he shook his head laughingly, telling them we didn't know any.

Finally the girls moved down the line to me. There I was, pouring with sweat, my breathing still slightly laboured, my fingers raw from my frenetic drumming. They peered at me through narrowed eyes, like I was a strange, alien lifeform. 'Erm,' they said hesitantly in an unsure tone of voice. 'Err . . . mmm . . . were you in the band?'

And that's when I realised: if you're the drummer you're barely a step up from a roadie in terms of visibility. You want to get noticed? Join a rock band. Just not as the drummer.

Except.

Tommy Lee is the drummer for Motley Crue. And he is, let's say, an exhibitionist. An outgoing, extrovert, attention-seeking individual. So we might phrase his 'problem' as 'When I'm on stage, how do I make sure the attention is on me?'

But he's got a constraint to add to the mix. 'When I'm on stage, how do I make sure the attention is on me . . . even though I'm at the back of the stage . . . sat behind an enormous drumkit?'

Just do a search on 'Tommy Lee spinning drumkit' or 'Tommy Lee rollercoaster drumkit' to find the answers. He worked around the constraint of being behind a drumkit and made it part of the solution – a more spectacular and unique solution than if he'd just stuck with the original problem of 'How do I make sure the attention is on me?' Which might have led to ideas where he got off from his drumkit and came to the front to compete with the vocalist and lead guitarist.

So how does using a constraint work? First, if you already have a problem, adding an additional constraint can disrupt the normal patterns of thinking. Suddenly you're thinking about the problem in a way that no one without the constraint is doing, so you're likely to get different answers than them. Even if you fail to fully overcome the constraint, you may still get exciting new answers to the original problem.

For instance, you might add to the problem, 'Oh, and it's got to be solved at zero cost'. That might seem crazy, and might even be ultimately unachievable, but that extra direction of now looking for 'free' solutions might set you down a new and successful path.

Secondly, if you don't have a 'real' problem but are just introducing a constraint which, if achieved, would create a real business benefit, you're giving your brain something to work with – a 'fun' problem to solve. Like a computer game that has a challenge to solve to get to the next level/area.

It gives you something to focus on and push against. 'OK, if we can't do that, then how about this?'

And it's a proven tool for achieving remarkable breakthroughs.

Action

BE CONSTRAINED TOOLKIT

1. Brainstorm some constraints you could introduce to the problem solving (or become problems of their own) or choose one from the examples given on page 47.

2. Ask which of those constraints might have an upside. Would adhering to that constraint be advantageous?

3. Whether your constraint has a clear benefit or is simply different, add it to the initial problem (if you had one) and brainstorm how to solve the problem now.

4. Because the constraint has been artificially created, it may not matter if you only partially achieve it, if it still gives you a great new solution to the original problem.

Four ways to constrain yourself

You begin by creating the constraint. To start with you could have a look at the ones below:

'The solution must cost nothing.'

'The solution must be implementable within a day.'

'The solution must be the first of its kind.'

'The solution must be popular.'

'The solution must be controversial.'

'The solution must remove an existing element.'

'The solution must not be technological.'

'The solution must not involve people.'

'The solution must make things simpler.'

You could also think up your own, very random constraints. 'The solution must have an edible element', or 'The solution must have a marine theme', or 'The solution must involve music', as suggested by the Igor Stravinsky quote at the beginning of this tool.

And you could look at other companies and products – either direct competitors or not – and 'borrow' one of their innovations to create a useful constraint. Such as 'Our solution must be ethical, like The Body Shop would do', or 'Our solution must involve fashion as Vogue would do'.

And finally, you could think of a constraint that would give you a competitive edge. Such as 'Solve the problem in a way that also reduces the cost to the customer'. Or 'Solve it in a way that also makes the product more robust'. Or 'Solve it so that it doubles the speed of the process'.

In fact, the next step is to look at the constraint and see if solving that too might have an obvious benefit.

For instance, if you were using the constraint, 'The solution must not be technological' you might say 'The benefit of that is, some of our competitors are more technologically advanced than us, so anything we came up with they'd copy and improve upon almost instantly'. Or 'The solution must not involve people' might suddenly get you solving your existing problem in a completely different way than you would have done, because now you're trying to do it without the final solution involving people at all – which might not only give you an unexpected answer, but one that's not subject to human error or costs.

PROBLEM-SOLVING TIP

Constraints are great when you haven't got a specific, urgent problem, but are just looking for greater business success. Like back when Apple launched the Macbook Air. 'Let's make the world's thinnest laptop.' They artificially constrained themselves to make their laptop thinner than anyone else's, not because they had a particular problem and not because that feature was in huge demand, but because it would give them a unique talking point for their product. They had to remove the mechanical hard drive and the optical drive to do it – but they got there.

Whatever constraint feels right to you will depend on the problem, obviously. It can be anything you want ultimately, just something that gives you a more specific line of attack for your brainstorm.

Tie them down to free them up

Once you've got your constraint, add it to the mix. You've tied everyone's hands: now see how they get on brainstorming the solution. In a way, it's the opposite of the *think bigger* tool. You're narrowing the thinking, and in part distracting their conscious mind (which, as we discovered in Part I: *Insight,* can work well).

Instead of discussing the problem, they'll be discussing the interesting new angle they've got to deal with. They'll explore how it can be achieved. And, perhaps, they'll get there.

It's like the movie *Apollo 13*. 'Houston, we have a problem.' During the movie (and sure, I know it's based on true events, but I'm sticking with the movie for my 'facts') there are a number of innovative solutions found to a whole host of problems they face. When they're cobbling together some new air scrubbers to reduce the CO_2 level in the air they're massively constrained as to what things they're able to use – so they have to be really creative with the solution (including using a sock as part of the filter).

It may sound strange, adding to a problem before trying to crack it, making it at first glance *more* difficult, but it really works. And as with many of the tools, you can use *be constrained* in conjunction with others. If adding a constraint alone doesn't stimulate people's thinking as much as you'd hoped, try solving the problem (with the constraint added) using another tool – like *choice architecture* or *interrogate and extrapolate.*

Example

Apple is a wonderful example of a company that gives itself constraints (or certainly used to, under Steve Jobs) in order to create breakthrough products and services.

I've already mentioned the Macbook Air, but what about the iPhone? Before it arrived, every single phone had a physical keypad. In fact, the idea of a phone without keys would have been laughable to every other manufacturer (like the then-dominant Nokia, Blackberry and Motorola). And to most customers too.

So there was no real problem to solve – people were happy with physical keys. They expected it. But Apple gave themselves an artificial constraint:

'What if we made a phone with *no* keypad?'

'Why would we want to do that?'

'Hmm. Good question. Well, if there was no keypad, there'd be more room for the screen.'

'And?'

'A bigger screen would mean it would be more useful for emails, web browsing, playing games . . .'

'Sounds good. But how do people make phone calls? Voice activation?'

'That could be one way.'

'But there'd still be times when you'd need to enter numbers and letters, like for texting.'

'OK, but if the whole phone is a screen . . . how about a virtual keypad, that just appears on the screen when you need it?'

'How would that work?

'Maybe we'd make the screen touch-sensitive.'

'Can we do that?'

'Hmm. Let's find out.'

In 2005, Apple bought a company called Fingerworks – experts in multi-touch surfaces. And on 9 January 2007, Steve Jobs revealed the iPhone to a gobsmacked world.

The negatives: the virtual keypad was not to everyone's taste. It was harder to use than a physical keypad, especially at first while you got used to the change.

The positives: a much bigger screen. The possibility for app icons – effectively buttons that you could customise and move around. Many *more* keys, because you get the (virtual) set you needed at any particular time. And of course, the fantastic experience of using a touch-sensitive screen for much more than pressing virtual keys; it was for swiping between screens, pinching to zoom in and out of webpages, touching to play games.

You could consider that achieving their constraint 'Let's make a new phone . . . with no keypad' was only a *partial* success. Because there still is a keypad – it's just that it's virtual, and only appears in cases when you need it. But that's the beauty of introducing a constraint: there's no absolute need to achieve it 100 per cent, it's a tool for changing your thinking or finding a new advantage.

Today it's hard to remember just what a groundbreaking idea a touchscreen phone was – and how it helped Apple leap ahead and dominate the mobile market in a very short space of time. (To the point where companies that kept physical buttons for a long time – like Blackberry – saw their business collapse.)

And it all began with a constraint. A constraint that, at first, could have been arbitrary. But which, when explored, would clearly provide some advantages. So they pursued it and pursued it and bought a company and developed a technology and launched a groundbreaking product that did something no other phone had done then . . . but which almost every phone does now.

Their kooky constraint has become *de rigueur* in the smartphone market.

Summary

Be constrained is a useful tool when the problem seems too open to solve, without any clear direction. Or when you don't have a specific, known opportunity, but are looking for an angle to then exploit.

To create an opportunity, come up with a powerful constraint to introduce to the status quo, and then explore what benefits it might have (like in the imagined Apple conversation in the example above).

That makes it different from the 'random insertion' tool described later (where you find a link with something random), because here you explore what possible *benefits* the constraint could have, and only once you've found one, proceed to use it.

Finally, to use *be constrained* successfully, ask:

- What constraint could we introduce? Either from the list under the toolkit for this tool, a competitor, our own imagination or specific to the particular problem (like keys on a phone)?

- What benefit might introducing that constraint create?

- Are we remembering that the aim is a great new solution/opportunity/innovation – so we don't have to actually implement the constraint part if we don't wish, it's just a thinking tool to help our brainstorming?

V.
Choice architecture

'I believe that if you show people the problems and you show them the solutions they will be moved to act.' BILL GATES

Many business problems arise simply because people are currently not acting in the way you need them to. Choice architecture is a powerful way to change that behaviour, by engineering the environment or circumstances so that the people concerned *want* to do the thing you want them to do.

Instead of trying to persuade them or cajole them or advise them or block off alternatives … you just make the course of action you want the most attractive option. *Et voilà*, problem solved.

Visual

For choice architecture, you're creating a pull (rather than the usual push). Look at the shaded area in the visual. That's the sweet spot for developing those kinds of answers, for designing the environment in which decisions are made.

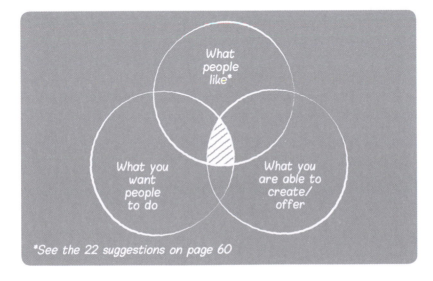

Theory

Choice architecture sounds fancy, but really it's as simple as constructing the environment so someone will choose the path you want them to choose. Or at the very least, *framing the options* in such a way so people choose the route you want them to.

It's a really positive, people-friendly way to arrange things. The people involved still feel like they have free choice, but you know they're going to choose the route you want them to take anyway. And as we all know, people will do things much more wholeheartedly and enthusiastically if it's something they *want* to do – especially if it's a choice they feel they came up with themselves.

The phrase *choice architecture* is used by Richard Thaler and Cass Sunstein in their fascinating book *Nudge*. They describe it as 'designing the context in which decision making happens', which is a great explanation.

Intelligent design, even in toilets

Choice architecture has become very popular in certain circles in recent years to describe the intelligent design of all sorts of physical and digital environments. And of course, the way things are designed can influence our choices, whether that choice is conscious or not, and whether the influencing design was done deliberately or not.

For instance, someone designing a ballot paper may not realise that the order the candidates appear in can affect the results. And the people filling out the ballot paper may not realise the order the candidates appear in can affect their choice.

Yet studies show that being first on the list in a ballot paper can get you 4 per cent more votes.

As a creative thinking tool, we can use *choice architecture* to solve problems by designing an environment or system which influences people's choices so the problem we had is negated. Or you can design an environment/system whereby people's new choices create an opportunity, or give you a competitive innovation.

It's perhaps best explained with an example, so let me take you to the men's toilets at Schiphol Airport (not literally).

There, they had a problem: men with, shall we say, 'poor aim syndrome' at the urinals (perhaps they were jetlagged). So, how could they get men to aim better?

Well, solving the problem: using the *choice architecture* tool means finding a solution where aiming well was something they *wanted* to do. Not something men were *cajoled* into or *warned* or just *informed* about. And it wasn't about solving the problem by making aiming *easier*.

So how do you make men *want* to aim better? In this case . . . by etching a realistic image of a fly on the urinal right near the plughole.

Men, being men, aimed for what looked like a real fly. They wanted to hit it. 'Poor aim syndrome' was solved and you can see flies etched on the urinals in Schiphol Airport to this day.

Not every problem or opportunity can be solved in this way, but many can. And it can be very powerful. It's a simple theory: it's obviously much easier to get people to do something that they themselves want to do.

Action

> CHOICE ARCHITECTURE TOOLKIT
>
> 1. Look at a problem that involves people.
>
> 2. Ask what it is that those people could do to negate the problem?
>
> 3. Now you have something quite different to brainstorm: how do we create (or present) an environment where people actively choose the route we want them to take?

As I say, *choice architecture* is about people, so it needs to be applied to a people-based problem/opportunity.

Then it's a matter of identifying what it is you really want those people to do for the problem to be solved. Think big: what would you really, really like them to do?

Once you know what you want from them, think about what they might want from you. Or from life. Or from the environment/system you're working in. Put yourself in their shoes and ask *What's In It For Me?* (WIIFM). Imagine that's all they're thinking.

Now, you just have to answer that question. What could be in it for them, to do the thing you want? You could incentivise it in some way, either financially or in some other tangible way. It feels a little bit like cheating, but it's OK.

Think positive: 22 starter ideas

Better still if you can find a way that appeals to people's heads or hearts. What positive thoughts can you conjure in them? What positive emotions? The bigger the thing you want them to do, the bigger the mental or emotional reward needs to be for them to still want to do it.

As a starter, things people want include: to have fun, to relax, to feel secure, to feel clever, to be popular, to be more successful, to be part of something good, to win, to be more attractive, to laugh, to feel joy, to do something worthwhile, to make a difference, to be recognised, to be thanked, to smile, to share, to eat something tasty, to experience something interesting or pleasurable or exciting or rewarding in some way.

You could go through each of these 22 ideas, for instance, and see how you could give your audience one of those experiences as a way to remove your problem or capitalise on your opportunity.

You can use the tool to be very clever (as in the escalator example I've put at the end) or you can use it really simply, in a fairly 'soft' way. For instance, if you're pitching to a client for a big piece of business, your problem might be 'How do we get these people to choose us over the competition?'

And you might traditionally spend all of your time and effort showing how your company is rationally and logically the best choice. You could just focus on how you'll meet/exceed their needs, how you have the right credentials and experience and so on.

Or . . . you could involve some *choice architecture*. Remembering that you'll be pitching face-to-face to real people, you could look at how you could make them *want* to choose you. As well as the rational business reasons, could you show you have the chemistry (both as a team and with the client) which will make working together more *fun*, or *rewarding* or *interesting*?

Could you convey the impression that not only will you do a great job, but if they choose you they'll look forward to every single meeting, because you make them 'feel good', compared to if they chose a competitor?

You've just created a different context for their decision making. (And believe me, people often choose companies they think they'll have a good relationship with over companies who might seem to be better technically, but with who they don't have the same positive emotional experience.)

So, as a starting point, how can you become the architect of a situation where the action you want people to take would give them one or more of the 22 things listed above? Or find other ways to engender your positive choice. Be inventive, be bold and persevere. As Einstein said, 'It's not that I'm so smart, it's just that I stay with a problem longer.'

PROBLEM-SOLVING TIP

Here's a simple bit of choice architecture: if you ever want a favour from someone, make sure you apologise first. A Harvard study by Alison Wood Brooks, Hengchen Dai and Maurice E. Schweitzer found that if a stranger at a train station on a rainy day asked people, 'Can I borrow your phone?' only 9 per cent said yes.

But if the stranger said 'I'm sorry about the rain! Can I borrow your phone?' 47 per cent said yes ('I'm sorry about the rain! Superfluous apologies demonstrate empathic concern and increase trust', *Social Psychological and Personality Science*, September 2013). A 'superfluous apology' – apologising unnecessarily for something which was obviously not their fault in the first place – had a dramatic effect, causing more than five times as many people to lend the apologist their phone. People wanted to help someone who said sorry to them – even when the apology was really rather meaningless.

Example

I've two for you – the first is Lloyds Bank, a client I worked with for a number of years along with Halifax. I gave a Halifax example for tool i, of how they *thought bigger* to create a unique savings product that would improve customer loyalty.

Let's look at the same area – bank savings accounts – for Lloyds.

They're a very different brand to Halifax, much more of a relationship brand and probably a bit more upmarket, so the prize draw idea for Halifax probably wouldn't suit Lloyds. But they have the same basic issue: they want to encourage their customers to save with them.

In fact, let's go further in the context of choice architecture: they want their customers to *want* to save with them. To enjoy doing so.

So they developed an online product they call *Money Manager*. It's really pretty simple: it automatically categorises your spending so you can see where your money goes (with a colourful pie chart breaking it down for you), and it lets you set up spending plans and savings goals. Which means you can set up a 'holiday' fund, for instance, set a target for it and watch yourself get closer to the target over time. There's even a calendar to show your progress month by month.

I'm not going to go so far as to say it makes saving *fun*, but it does make it more tangible and meaningful for many people. It may encourage Lloyds customers to save more. And it certainly may encourage more casual savers to do so with Lloyds, using the Money Manager service, without Lloyds having to rely on having the best savings rate to attract those customers.

So a completely different solution using a completely different tool to the Halifax's *Savers Prize Draw*, but with the same enviable result: more customers who are more loyal.

Here's my second example, Volkswagen, which has pursued the idea of *choice architecture* with its 'Fun Theory' series you can find on YouTube. It's now grown into an event where lots of people are solving 'real-world' problems with choice architecture.

One of the first ideas involved the escalators on the Swedish underground. The video you'll find on YouTube shows an escalator next to the (quite short) staircase. Everyone's using the escalator, no one's bothering with the stairs. So the problem was: how do we get more people to use the stairs? Because using the stairs would be a good thing – it would free the escalator up for people with bags or small children or who were pregnant or infirm or elderly.

Using other creative thinking tools, all sorts of solutions could have come up, such as putting up signs saying, 'Please save the escalators for the old, infirm or pregnant'. Or signs saying, 'Using the stairs burns off 20 calories'. Or turning the escalator off, or making it really slow.

But they didn't do any of those things. They used *choice architecture* to come up with an idea that would make people *want* to use the stairs rather than the escalator.

So, overnight, they turned the stairs into a giant working keyboard. Every step a different note in the scale. And the next day, many, many more people chose to use the stairs, because it was suddenly more enjoyable than using the escalator.

Summary

Choice architecture is useful for solving organisational issues that involve people. Behavioural problems, you might call them. It can also be used as an opportunity in the same way – you might not have a significant issue, but you could still see a significant benefit of getting many more people to behave in a certain way.

You're just looking at ways to create an environment where people still have free will, but you make your desired choice their preferred choice too, by finding a way to make it more rewarding or pleasurable or easier or in some unexpected way better than the alternative.

To use *choice architecture* successfully, ask:

- How could we harness people (whether staff, customers, the general public, advocates or competitors) to solve our problem?

- How could we appeal to these people's heads and hearts? What would they like?

- If people are choosing option A rather than our desired option B, how can we make option B more desirable to them? What would make it more beneficial or rewarding or pleasurable or interesting or quicker or easier or more enjoyable?

- Can we have fun with it? Are we remembering that powerful change can be affected simply by making the choice we want – however serious it is – more fun to do? (Like where people set up a speed camera lottery – everyone who went under the speed limit was entered into a prize draw to win the fines from the people who broke the speed limit. A fun solution to a serious issue, and incredibly successful.)

vi.
Old + old = new

'An idea is nothing more, nor less, than a new combination of old elements.' JAMES WEBB YOUNG

There's a little book called *A Technique for Producing Ideas* (catchy, I know) by James Webb Young where he puts forward the above hypothesis.

Now I don't know if that's *always* the case, but I do know that combining existing ingredients can create a brand new recipe. And *old + old = new* can be particularly effective for developing new opportunities, but it can also be valuable for some kinds of problem solving too.

Visual

Block A means you can only go up three levels. Block B means you can travel a further distance, but only go up two levels. But put them together and you create something new that lets you go up five levels.

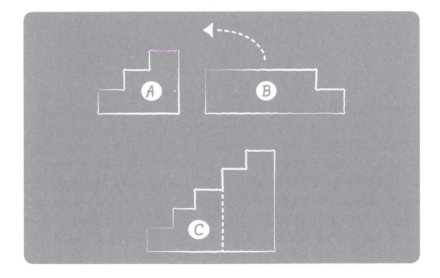

Theory

Combining existing ideas to create something new is an activity our brains are very good at – which is one reason why it's a good starting point for problem solving and innovating.

We find it relatively easy, compared to some of the tools here. Many jokes are the result of taking existing elements and combining them. And many inventions are too. Trevor Baylis put together clockwork and radio. What amazes me most is that he did it in 1991 – radio had been around for 100 years by then. Clockwork for 2,000. Yet not until 1991 was the wind-up radio developed.

What is cloud computing, other than the existing idea of securely storing computer data and the existing idea of webmail? In fact, before cloud storage became popular, I would sometimes attach a file to an email and save the email in my drafts, just so I could log onto my email from another computer and access the file from there.

What's a *mashup*? Just two existing songs brought together to create something new. Or, on the web, a mashup is pulling in existing content from different sources, combined to create something new.

And in science, different disciplines working together to make a breakthrough is a proven route to success. In fact, after decades of scientific disciplines becoming more discrete and specialist, there has been a move in recent years to introduce more cross-disciplinary thinking (like the Johns Hopkins Science of Learning Institute). Promising innovations like bionanotechnology, for instance, are only possible thanks to people in different fields bringing together their existing knowledge to meet challenges (or make opportunities) in a new way.

Clearly as a starting point it's easier for the brain to work with something that's put in front of it than to work from a blank sheet of paper.

It's also useful to work with things that are already, individually, successful and useful.

And, because the brain is so good at finding patterns and connections and bringing things together, it can often combine those existing ideas to create something new.

Action

OLD + OLD = NEW TOOLKIT

1. You can begin with what you already have/the way things are as one of your old ideas that you're going to combine with something else.

2. You can combine more than two ideas – try two, three or perhaps even four.

3. Brainstorm what good and useful existing ideas are already 'out there' that you'd like to integrate to create something new.

4. Sense-check that by bringing more than one idea, you really are creating something new, not simply stacking up existing ideas without changing them.

5. And check that the new idea is as simple as the original ideas were: it's easy to combine elements to create something complex and convoluted, but that's rarely very useful.

There are a number of ways to use this tool according to whether you're looking at a problem or an opportunity.

First approach – use an existing element

Let's look at Trevor Baylis's invention again. He did it as a response to a problem: he saw a programme on TV about the spread of AIDS. And about how information would make a big difference: informing affected communities in the developing world. Radio would be perfect; except there was no electricity and batteries wouldn't last very long.

We could say the problem was 'Radios won't work because mains power or batteries aren't an option'. So Trevor took the 'old' or existing part of the problem (the radio) and combined it with an existing area of power that wasn't electricity or batteries: clockwork. He was then left with the practical, technical aspects of creating a clockwork, wind-up system that could power a radio.

So the starting point there is to use a key element from the existing problem, magically add something existing from somewhere else that would solve the problem, and find a way of integrating them.

(Nowadays in some rural parts of the developing world they have solar charging stations that use solar energy to power rechargeable batteries which can then be used in any battery-powered appliance.)

Second approach – use entirely new elements

When you're innovating, you may just want to start with two (or three, or four) things that already exist, but which aren't necessarily part of your company's existing portfolio. It may be two things that are particularly desirable or effective in their own fields. It's a step on from just plucking desirable *qualities* out of the air and trying to create those. So you might say 'I want a vehicle that's as small and easy to park as a *motorbike*, but with the roof and boot of a *car*', and you might have come up with the Smart car. Which, like a motorbike, can reverse up to the kerb to park, meaning it can get into very small spaces.

In fact, the Smart car was the brainchild of the CEO of Swatch (SMART is an acronym of Swatch Mercedes Art).

PROBLEM-SOLVING TIP

In chemistry, you can add elements to create either a *mixture* or a *combination*. A mixture is where two or more elements are blended together but each element remains unchanged. Whereas a combination is something entirely new, where the elements have reacted to create a new substance. Think: is your new idea a *mixture* or a *combination*? Generally, a combination is what you're looking for; a way of making the existing parts interact to create something completely fresh. Whereas a mixture of two old ideas … is just two old ideas.

A word of caution: sense-check what you've created, especially if it's a new service or product. There have been plenty of product launches over the years where people have combined existing ideas to create something new . . . that nobody wanted.

And you wonder who ever thought there would be a market for them. The toaster radio, anyone? Yes, they do still exist and you can still buy them ... but without offering any clear benefit over having a free choice of radio and toaster. They've taken ubiquitous kitchen items and created something extremely niche – and so unlikely to be very profitable.

Example

Some people are willing to say things on the phone that they're not as keen to put in an email. They like the fact that (unless you're being wiretapped by MI5), the phone call is ephemeral.

The other person can remember what you said, but they don't have a physical record of it. So you speak more freely than you might in an email or even a text, where you're likely to be a bit more guarded and scrutinise what you're saying.

But ... what if you could combine that age-old way of intangible communication with another old idea: sending phone pics?

That would give you something new: Snapchat.

It's a really simple idea – use the Snapchat app to send photos (with captions) to your friends. But the photos are automatically deleted from their view after a period you set.

The way the app operates to send photos means it also works over WiFi. Which allows you to send pictures without using up your data plan if you're connected to WiFi, and also means you can send pics from things other than a smartphone (like a tablet). These are a couple of handy benefits that helped the app take off in the early days, but which weren't necessarily in the thinking of the people who developed it; they were bonus benefits that the community of (young) users worked out.

Anyway, Snapchat is a good example of taking two very simple, old ideas and mashing them together to create a simple, new idea.

Sending pictures – old idea.

Communication that's of the moment and of which there's no physical record – old idea.

Sending pictures 'in the moment' while leaving no lasting record of them – new idea.

It's a creation that might only seem to appeal to a rather niche market – generally, young people who like sending dodgy images to one another, often 'selfies'.

But think about that for a moment: most young people love social, digital communication. They don't want to bother having to write long streams of prose to communicate. And they love being rude and lewd among their friends. In other words, across the world you've got a huge 'niche' market.

And with online trolls and 'cyberbullying' rife, a way of sending pictures and text that leaves no trace is very attractive to them.

At the time of writing, Snapchat delivers more than 200 million images every day. And Facebook was allegedly willing to pay over $3 billion to buy the company just two years after it launched.

Which by my maths means Snapchat's value has grown, in its very short lifetime, at a rate of about £3 million a day. Just by smashing together two old ideas.

Summary

Old + old = new is a well-established, easy-to-follow creative thinking tool. It's particularly easy to use for innovating, creating a new opportunity by putting existing elements together (as in the Snapchat example).

But it's also useful for solving problems, as with the clockwork radio. What makes it so useful as a tool is that you're simply bringing together existing elements, so you don't need to come up with something brand new. Which is not only easier, it's also likely to be more palatable to the business, as it seems *less* new and therefore less unknown and risky.

Finally, to use *old + old = new* successfully, ask:

- For problem solving: what is the important element from our existing circumstance we need to keep? What existing element from 'out there' could we introduce, to solve the current problem? OK, so how do we integrate them?

- Are we looking wide enough – across different sectors, industries, cultures and disciplines – to find new but existing elements we could introduce?

- What effect would we like to achieve? What exists out there that does that? How could we adapt that to work for us? (Like with the radio: 'What form of power already exists that isn't battery or electricity and which is cheap and robust? Clockwork.')

- For innovating: what different existing things have desirable qualities we'd like? In which case, can we find a way to integrate those existing things?

- Are we *combining* old elements (to create something genuinely new) rather than just *adding* elements that don't really interact?

- Are we combining the right things? The right number of things? What's like item X that we've introduced, but not quite the same? Would that have a better effect?

- Are we keeping the result as simple as possible and not getting needlessly complex?

vii.
Reverse engineering

'One man's magic is another man's engineering.' ROBERT HEINLEIN

Reverse engineering is a term generally used to describe taking apart a 'thing' (whether mechanical or technological) that you didn't create, in order to understand how it works so that you can then create a replica of your own.

A famous example is cracking the Enigma code in World War II – a brilliant piece of reverse engineering by cryptologists.

Here I mean something slightly different. In problem solving, we can reverse engineer from the solution. In other words, start at the end – with the solution or innovation you want – and work backwards from there.

Visual

The visual shows some of the elements of your business. Working out how to get them to fit together seamlessly is a difficult puzzle, likely to involve trial and error and take an age. But when you've seen what success looks like (the square underneath), reverse engineering from there to put every individual piece in the right place becomes a straightforward copying process.

Theory

Consider this joke, voted best at the Edinburgh Festival one year. 'I've heard a rumour that Cadbury's are bringing out a new chocolate bar for the Asian market. It could be a Chinese Wispa.' It's a simple play on words, making a joke out of the fact 'whisper' can be used two different ways.

You could create lots of new jokes with exactly the same method. I've just Googled 'clichés' to give me an existing phrase. Here's my joke using it:

'I didn't have much time for dinner last night, so I just poured it into a padded envelope. I ate it *in a jiffy*.' OK, it's a terrible joke. OK, it's barely a joke. But I thought it up just now, in about 20 seconds, after looking at the phrase 'in a jiffy'.

The point is, you can work backwards from your end point with punning jokes, with encrypted war commands . . . and with business solutions.

The benefit of hindsight

Implicit in this tool is the idea that it's easier to achieve a goal once you know that goal *is* achievable. Once Edison had cracked the lightbulb, other people knew it was worth working on too, because they knew it was possible. Before then, well, it might have been impossible for all anyone knew – and that can be demotivating.

So our theory of reverse engineering is that once we know what we want the solution to be – and that solution sounds plausible and realistic – our brains are perfectly capable of stepping backwards from that end point all the way to where we currently are. And then just reversing the steps.

Action

> **REVERSE ENGINEERING TOOLKIT**
>
> 1. Start at the end: what does the ideal solution look like? Ignore the problem for the time being and focus on what the outcome you want is.
>
> 2. Gradually step away from that position, so you move from where you want to be to where you are, looking at the changes, in reverse order, required to get there.
>
> 3. Now look at these steps in order of from where you are to where you want to be, and establish the actions needed to execute them.

This tool has a lovely starting point: you simply ask what would you *like* to be the case? What would be the dream position, the way you'd love things to be? Write that out, big and bold, for everyone to see and agree.

And instead of focusing on solving a problem, suddenly you're focusing on achieving a solution.

> **PROBLEM-SOLVING TIP**
>
> Sometimes you won't know what the solution might look like, and that's when other tools will serve you better, to help you find that answer. But other times, you might already have in mind what you want the world to look like. That's the time when taking this approach will work for you.

Step by step

There are then two simple ways to look at reverse engineering from your end point – one, as mentioned in the theory, is to work backwards, step by step. Start stepping away, looking at the things you need to begin, change or stop to achieve those steps. Keep stepping further and further out until your reverse-engineered solution meets your current problem, and you know what needs doing to get from the problem to the solution.

So, to be really simplistic, if you came to the view that the solution to your problem was a column that was 100 bricks high, working backwards, you'd decide that the step before that was to have a column 99 bricks high. The step before that, one 98 bricks high. The step before that . . . and so on, until you've gone through all the steps backwards to where you currently are.

Then you can just reverse the order to solve the problem and achieve your goal. In that particular example, by finding 100 bricks.

Holistic approach

The other way to reverse engineer is not to work in a logical one-step-back-at-a-time way, but look at the whole picture and see if it's possible to engineer the whole environment or system or process to achieve that end point. Dismantle every barrier. Change things so that not only *can* your dream end point happen, it *does* happen. Even if you don't achieve it 100 per cent, you should improve things dramatically.

Either way, it's a very simple tool – effectively, instead of starting with the problem and looking at how to 'fix' it, you ignore the problem, and jump straight to how you want the world to be. Instead of 'Some customers are unhappy because they're not receiving their order within 72 hours', you're focusing on your ideal, perhaps 'Every customer gets their order in 48 hours'. Now you just look at what you need to do to make that a reality – at which point you may turn to some of the other creative thinking tools in this book to help.

And it may mean you don't have to deal with the original issue or challenge at all, because you've found a completely new way to achieve your ambitions.

Example

Here's a story someone who used to work at Boden told me.

They had an objective: maximise their sales. That was the end point. So how could they reverse-engineer from 'their best sales ever' to create the environment for that to happen?

One approach was to look at their previous best sales occasions, and work backwards to see how those occasions came about, so they could replicate them.

One such instance happened when they featured, in their Mini Boden catalogue (for children), a Sheriff T-shirt. Although, while it was *called* a Sheriff T-shirt, it was actually a child's T-shirt with a picture of a gun on the front (a cowboy gun).

Gun crime

A lot of customers complained. Boden was selling children's T-shirts with pictures of guns on the front! The Bodenites were enraged.

So Boden did the right thing: they apologised. Unreservedly. In fact, customers got a personal email from Johnnie Boden, which included the line, 'We made a mistake with this product and we feel stupid – especially me. Please accept my apologies.' He also said, 'Keep the feedback coming, good or bad. It's the only way we can get better.'

Not every customer got the email, but thanks to social media, many more found out about it.

But here's the thing. Apparently, the following catalogue had spectacular sales. The woman I spoke to said it seemed like being honest and apologising promptly and promising to put things right had actually increased customer loyalty. People were impressed.

To the point where some people at Boden, looking at reverse engineering their great sales . . . were wondering if maybe they shouldn't deliberately make *another* mistake of some kind, which they could then apologise for. (They didn't go through with it, but it's an interesting idea.)

Rubbing his nose in it

Here's one more reverse engineering story for you. The version I've heard concerns a businessman named Tim Martin. So let's start at the end: he wants to rub a former teacher's nose in his success.

Why? Because that teacher had told him that he'd never be a success, that he'd never make it in business. So Tim wants to prove him wrong. Again and again and again. A frequent reminder of the man's mistaken negativity.

So how do we reverse engineer from that point, with a businessman who owns 540 pub restaurants around the country?

In this case, by businessman Tim Martin naming those pub restaurants not after himself, but after his 'inspiration' – the teacher who said he wouldn't make it. So that the teacher would see his own name everywhere he went, but know that he didn't own any of the places bearing his name. They weren't his successes, but those of the student he'd slighted.

And that teacher's name was Mr J. D. Wetherspoon.

Summary

Reverse engineering is a useful tool when you're able to visualise the solution you want. Many times you won't, and one of the other tools will help you come up with a solution you hadn't previously considered. But when you know the answer to your problem, reverse engineering can help you work out how to achieve it.

It's the same with an opportunity or innovation – you might have already had a brilliant innovation idea; now you just want to work out how to develop it. And one answer is by working backwards; whether step by step or by looking at the whole thing and debating what you need to do to your business to create the solution you've envisaged.

To use *reverse engineering* successfully, ask:

- Are we focusing on a problem obsessively when instead we could be just looking at what we'd like to be the case – what we want the world to be like?

- If our world did look like that, how did we get there? Let's move back from that future, step by step, to the present, noting all the retrograde changes along the way so we can then reverse the steps to get to that ideal future.

- What if we look at someone else? What other company (perhaps in another field) is achieving the success we want? How do they do it? How do they operate? How can we move back, step by step, from where they are to where we are, and then reverse the process in implementation, to take our business to where theirs is?

viii.
Sidestep the issue

'When life gives you lemons, make lemonade.'

It's like the old joke, 'My arm hurts in several places.' 'Well, stop going to those places then.'

You've got a problem/challenge/issue? Well, instead of trying to solve it, just create an environment where it doesn't matter.

Visual

We automatically start trying to solve a problem, when we might just be able to sidestep it. Instead of trying to find our way around the maze, we can sidestep the whole navigation nightmare. We'll ignore that problem, but still achieve our goal by simply cutting a hole in the hedge instead. It's quicker and easier, playing by our own rules.

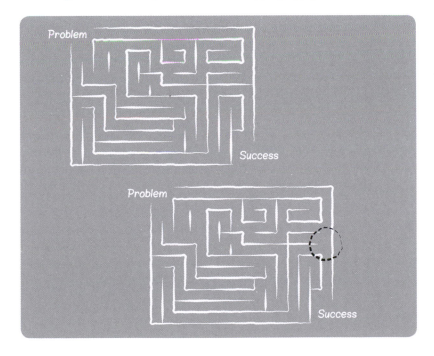

Theory

Given a problem, our brain will start trying to solve it. A crossword, a Sudoku, how to make text wrap around an image in PowerPoint, how to make spag bol without three of the ingredients, how to reclaim the armrest from the train passenger next to you.

Our brain can't help it: it sees a problem, it dives in. Clever three pounds of nerve cells.

On the other hand, it doesn't stop to ask: is this problem *worth* solving? Foolish lump of grey gristle.

You can scale an individual brain up to a big business too. Problems Must Be Solved. It's our default position. Except ... maybe they don't have to be. Maybe instead of working out a way to remove the huge great boulder in your path ... you could just walk round it.

It's like this: if your toaster breaks, you could try to fix it. You could start by changing the fuse, you could give it a good clean, you could check all the connections, you could look up toaster repairs on the internet, you could even – as a last resort – refer to the manual. And you could solve the problem of a broken toaster by getting a new one, obviously.

But if 'I have a broken toaster' is the problem, instead of solving it by buying a new toaster, how could you sidestep the issue instead? Stop having toast, for one thing. Or grill your bread. Or use a toasting fork and do your toasting on the hob or the fire. Use that grilled sandwich maker languishing in the back of the cupboard. Start using the local café. Or buy French toast.

You see? Start exploring alternatives or ways around the problem, rather than just tackling it head on and you can come up with some really interesting ideas that otherwise might never have occurred to you. I mean: *French toast.*

Action

> ## SIDESTEP THE ISSUE TOOLKIT
>
> 1. Look at the problem and ask what the consequences of not fixing it are: what's the cost/benefit ratio?
>
> 2. Explore ways around the problem, so you can still get to the same place without engaging the problem.
>
> 3. Also explore alternatives where you take a radically different direction which makes the whole issue irrelevant.

You've got the problem written out large on the wall somewhere. Remind everyone of it. Now a bit of role play: imagine you're all walking along a narrow path with sheer cliffs either side. And the problem is a giant granite boulder right bang in your way. It's 20 foot high. It's been there 1,000 years. It's impervious to dynamite and it's too smooth to climb.

You're going to have to find a way to squeeze around the boulder, or you're going to have to find an alternative route. Removing the boulder or changing it in some way is not an option.

Getting everyone to think like that can help people understand the nature of this tool. There are other tools you will use/have used that have been about tackling the boulder – this is about getting around it.

The toolkit on the visual aid goes through the three simple steps of the *sidestep the issue* tool.

You begin by asking, 'How big a problem is it? What's the cost, impact, consequences of it?' Ask these questions not because you might decide, 'Oh let's not bother then': it's unlikely to be a trivial issue else you wouldn't be running the session in the first place. No, looking at the effects of the problem can often give you a way around it. Like with my silly toaster example: the consequences of a broken toaster are you can't make toast. And immediately two things occur: yes you can, here are three other ways to make toast without a toaster. Or, well who cares about toast – I prefer bagels. And they never used to fit in the toaster anyway.

The next two steps are different ways to use the tool.

The first: find ways of making the problem irrelevant, as in the Stella example that follows. What could you change in the process or the environment or other factor that would mean the problem was no longer a problem? Instead of clearing the blockage, just make it meaningless. Change the game. In the case of the boulder example, you've decided that the goal should be climbing the cliffs, so it doesn't matter whether there's a boulder in the path or not.

Stella profits

Companies do this all the time in their marketing, positioning and advertising. Look at Stella Artois: their lager wasn't the cheapest, and perhaps customers didn't know why they should pay more for one pint of mass-produced lager than another. So the problem could have been presented as 'How do we make our lager cheaper?' Or even 'How do we prove our more costly lager tastes better?' But they simply sidestepped both those issues with the strapline *Reassuringly expensive*. Instead of removing the 'higher price' boulder they gave it a big hug and said 'Look at our lovely boulder' (positioning the disadvantage as an advantage – a bit like the Guinness example we looked at in the *Problem solving solved* introduction).

They did it again years later: there was a resurgence in the cider market, led by Magners, and Stella Artois wanted to join the party. But they were late to what had become a very crowded, competitive cider market. So they sidestepped the issue of being just another cider ... by calling their product *cidre*. It fitted beautifully with the French advertising, the campaign leading with the idea of, 'It's not cider, it's cidre'. And in the space of a couple of years, Stella Artois' *cidre* became a major player, even outselling Magners.

Just by finding a way around the problem. Instead of competing in the cider category, they invented a new one: *cidre*. Which might sound like a superficial marketing gimmick – and in many ways it is – but it was very, very successful.

The second: find alternative ways to leave the problem untouched and find an alternative route to get to the original goal. In the boulder analogy, you turn away from the obstacle and look for a completely different route to get to where you want to be. It might take longer, but it may be more scenic. Or, it might take longer, but it still involves less time and effort than removing the boulder would.

So start working together to ask, 'How do we get to where we want to be without engaging the problem at all? What's a completely new way to get there?' You may come up with a new method that no one else is doing, that gives you a real breakthrough and competitive edge.

It's a bit like that difficult colleague I mentioned earlier, who you need to sign off on something. Instead of trying to solve the problem of winning them over, you could just change the proposal you have so it doesn't need their sign off (route 1: sidestep the issue by changing the game). Or you wait until they're on holiday and get their boss to sign it off instead (route 2: sidestep the issue by finding a new route to the objective).

As I've said before, using different creative thinking tools can sometimes lead to the same answer – and you might have got to the 'Get their boss to sign it off instead' solution by using one of the other tools in this section. But there are occasions when trying to sidestep the problem, rather than find a novel solution for it, can yield answers that are simple, useful and, in retrospect, blindingly obvious.

Example

Here's a great story I've heard about a yoghurt company that had a problem with shelf life.

Namely that it wasn't long enough. If they could make their product last longer, they wouldn't get as much wastage. They wouldn't have to supply supermarkets as frequently. They'd save a lot of money. Making it both a problem and an opportunity.

So the boss pushed the yoghurt company's scientists to find ways to make the fruit yoghurt last longer, to push the 'Best before' date ever further away.

But there was a limit to what they could do. After all, you're talking about dairy yoghurt mixed with acidic fruit. They're going to react with each other and ultimately the yoghurt will spoil. Which, when they reached the limit of what they could achieve, is what the scientists told the boss.

Hmm, said the boss. So the problem is how to make the yoghurt last longer. But you say the cause of the problem is that the fruit and the yoghurt are reacting together?

So let's just sidestep the issue.

Instead of finding a way to make the yoghurt and fruit last longer together ... we won't put them together. We'll sell the yoghurt with the fruit kept separate, in its own little corner compartment.

And the customer puts them together when they're ready to eat it.

And lo! The longer-lasting-yoghurt-with-fruit-in-a-separate-corner-tray was born.

Instead of solving the original problem, they just found a way around it. All those scientists could stop trying to find ingenious additives to make the two key ingredients sit happily together. Just don't put them together. Sidestep the issue.

Then, it was just a matter of marketing. Don't tell people that the yoghurt and the fruit are kept separate to make it last longer. Tell them it's so they get to mix them together however they want.

Genius.

Summary

Sidestep the issue is a useful tool when you suspect the problem cannot be removed or even significantly altered. (You might be wrong, of course – don't assume that it can't be removed and that therefore this is the only useful tool. Many challenges that businesses believed were insurmountable, others proved otherwise – and stole a march on their competitors as a result. As Henry Ford said, 'Whether you think you can or you can't, you're right'.)

But it is a handy approach for finding a way to get around a problem with less time, money or manpower.

To use *sidestep the issue* successfully, ask:

- Are we assuming that because we have a problem, we need to solve it – when actually, we could change the goal, or work around it?

- How can we work around it? What can we change in our process or environment or market or people or attitude or something else which means the original problem is still there, but we find another route to the same goal?

- Or, can we reframe the challenge? Think about it in a different way so it's not the same goal – like Stella introducing '*cidre*' to sidestep the problem of competing in the cider category?

ix.
Random insertion

'Thinking is the hardest work there is, which is probably the reason so few people engage in it.' HENRY FORD

We couldn't look at problem solving without considering lateral thinking, the term popularised by Edward de Bono.

It's a way to 'jump the tracks' when we all start thinking along the same lines, solving problems the same old way.

The particular approach to lateral thinking I'm going to cover here uses aleatoricism (don't ask me how it's pronounced), which means using randomness. 'The introduction of chance into the act of creation.' I'll just call it *random insertion*.

Visual

Ask someone to think of a number from 1 to 50 – there's your random word to use. Or if you have the table printed out big, get someone to close their eyes and put a finger on the table.

1 elephant	2 secret	3 tea bag	4 shoe
5 sleeping bag	6 hair	7 stapler	8 pizza
9 bed	10 wheel	11 suitcase	12 beard
13 leaf	14 balloon	15 yellow	16 firework
17 wings	18 starfish	19 flamingo	20 castle
21 spear	22 taxi	23 motorbike	24 apple
25 camera	26 poker	27 cardigan	28 speaker
29 peanut butter	30 drumkit	31 windmill	32 drill
33 dustbin	34 plaster	35 soft	36 prison
37 flume	38 aluminium	39 shark	40 charcoal
41 butler	42 wellies	43 mirror	44 hole
45 chip shop	46 statue	47 periscope	48 button
49 axe	50 trombone		

Theory

This is something we looked at back in Part I: *Insight*. Namely, that the only way our poor overburdened brain can survive in this insanely complex, stimulus-heavy world is to find some shortcuts. It can't think about everything from scratch every time. Imagine if your brain insisted on tackling shoelace-tying with fresh aplomb every morning. 'There must be a better way,' it says in earnest, making your fingers experiment with a hundred different knotting combinations. You'd never get to work on time. Or at all.

Our brains have a variety of brilliant tricks for coping with the enormity facing them every day, and autopilot and pattern-recognition are two of them. When we've got something that seems to work, we stick with it. We don't keep investigating and exploring new things.

How to become a chess master

We get stupendously good at recognising patterns, and using that recognition to guide our next step. It's how chess Grandmasters become Grandmasters (like Garry Kasparov, who I mentioned in *Insight*). They play so many games that their brains start to recognise and recall board layouts. They can see the pattern, and can draw upon the experience of those previous games to know what's a strong move from that position.

But, when you're trying to make a leap forward into uncharted territory (solving a problem you've never solved before, or developing a new innovation, for instance), a brain that only relies on what's gone before is going to be limited.

If your brain relies on previous patterns, it's going to come up with previous answers. Which presumably weren't successful, otherwise you wouldn't be holding your problem-solving session.

But if we give that system a jolt, by introducing something unexpected – a random insertion – into the mix, then letting our brain find an association between the current situation and that, well then. Now we've got a bit of magic going on. Now our brain's brilliant ability to find connections and make patterns is working for innovation, not against it.

PROBLEM-SOLVING TIP

Try the 'Mad Inventor' exercise to get people thinking laterally. Split the group into teams of two or three. Each team has three pieces of paper. On the first they write down the name of an object (the *fact*). On the second they write down what it looks like (its *form*). On the third they write what it does (its *function*). Now you create three piles, *Fact*, *Form* and *Function*. Shuffle each pile. And now each team takes one fact, one form and one function at random and invents something that does all three.

So one group might end up with 'camera', 'for digging holes in the ground' and 'soft and yellow'. Can you invent a soft and yellow camera that would be useful when digging holes in the ground? Congratulations, you're the latest winner on *Dragons' Den*. But more importantly, you've thought laterally: forced your brain to find a connection and relationship between ideas you'd never have put together without random intervention.

Action

RANDOM INSERTION TOOLKIT

1. Use a dictionary or other 'simple noun generator' to create a seed word, plus the broader term which describes it, and an attribute it has.

2. Use those three words as springboards to solve your problem, such as finding an association between the word and your problem; you may generate a 'bridging idea' first.

3. Alternatively, come up with an interesting idea or fact from the list of supplied categories (giving you more control over the seed word), and see if you can find a useful link between that and your goal.

There are two ways I suggest you use random insertion. Both revolve around taking your original problem/opportunity and adding an element not normally associated with it, to inspire unexpected answers.

Be really random

The first route is to pick a word, at random (unsurprisingly). You can use whatever source you like for this; some are suggested on the visual aid, or alternatively use a dictionary or a catalogue – I've always found the Argos catalogue (or 'Laminated Book of Dreams', as I remember comedian Bill Bailey calling it) to be pretty useful.

PROBLEM-SOLVING TIP

Generally stick with simple, concrete nouns for your seed word. Things like shoe, balloon, apple, plaster. Complex or abstract nouns, or verbs or adjectives, will usually be a lot more difficult to work with, because they're more difficult for our minds to visualise.

Choose a page at random, close your eyes and stick a finger on the page. See what you land on.

WHAT DOES A SLEEPING BAG MAKE YOU THINK OF?
Write the word up on the flipchart. Also write up the broader category it belongs to. And a third word: an attribute of that thing. So you might have flicked to the camping page of the Argos catalogue, and your finger might have landed on a sleeping bag. So you'd write *sleeping bag*, and the broader term, *sleeping* and an attribute of a sleeping bag, like *snug* or *warm*.

Alternatively, you can write up the seed word *sleeping bag* and then ask people to say words they associate with it, like *zip* or *tents* or *scouts* or *Glastonbury*. Write three of these up instead, if you wish. Either way, you've now got three words for everyone to look at, plus the original problem/opportunity.

Now you can use any of the three words to solve your problem – giving you a different kind of constraint ('Your solution must be related to zips' kind of thing). It's forcing your brain to come up with an association between the problem/innovation and one of your words, giving you ideas you might never have otherwise had.

You may need to go back and research any involvement (however loose) the word might have with the background to your problem – some solutions require a detailed knowledge of the background in order to be 'solved' or worked around.

BRIDGING IDEA
I should also mention an intermediate stage you may use: developing a bridging idea to help the group in your session. Just take one of your seed words and look at how one of its attributes might be relevant to the problem. Then brainstorm around that. For instance, let's say your problem is, 'We haven't got enough people to answer every phone call within our three minute service promise'. One of your random words is *cake*. So you say OK, an attribute of cake is that it tastes good. That's our bridging idea. So what might we do to make *not* calling feel good for the customer, or only talking on the phone for a very short space of time feel good for the customer?

And suddenly people are brainstorming ideas where customers are encouraged and rewarded to email instead of call, or their call is free provided it's under five minutes long or you create a FAQs guide that's a fantastically entertaining pop-up book which means customers enjoy reading it, and having done so have much better knowledge – so fewer of them call to ask questions they could have found in the product guide in the first place.

Now you're getting fewer calls and so are able to answer them more easily (and therefore faster).

> **PROBLEM-SOLVING TIP**
>
> Random insertion is not always easy. I must say that; groups often struggle with this tool. It can feel very alien, and it can certainly be difficult to make quick progress, so people get discouraged. You might find a link, but not a way for that link to be a helpful solution. But persevere. A great solution is out there, and it is zip-based (or whatever random words you have). You've just got to push through the mental stitch until you get your second wind and the ideas start flowing.

Be semi-random

The second version of this tool is to be slightly less random. Instead of using a dictionary/catalogue/Google's 'I'm feeling lucky' search, anyone in the group can suggest something, based on the following categories: nature, recent conversations, the news, culture, science, sport, nature, travel, technology, history, hobbies.

That way, people are suggesting words they have a vested interest in (because they chose them). It also means they're coming up with words which, for whatever reason, are currently resonating quite strongly with them. Either because they've recently come into contact with that subject (recency being a strong factor in recall) or because it's something that feels very important or interesting to them, so it's on their mind.

Whatever the reason, it can make the brainstorming team feel more engaged with the process when the seed word is one they've come up with, rather than one that random chance has imposed on them. Just use the categories above (also on the visual aid) to prompt ideas for words.

As I said, this tool doesn't always feel natural for some people. But nothing good comes easy, as they say. And you'll certainly find this tool a useful springboard for innovation sessions; it really opens your mind to just how creative you can be when you force your brain to 'jump the tracks'.

Example

Let me go back to the master of lateral thinking, Mr de Bono. He was asked by the Foreign Office to think about a solution to the Middle East crisis.

So, Edward de Bono is (let us imagine) looking at all the issues in the Middle East, all the politics, history, cultural and religious reasons behind the conflicts and instability.

And he's looking to solve the issue with a simple, radical solution that no one else has thought of. So, using random insertion, one of the seed words he comes up with is *banana*.

He writes that down, and the broader term behind it, *food*, and also an attribute of it *nourishes you*.

Let's say, exploring the idea of nourishing, he thinks about how comforting a bowl of hot soup can be – maybe the answer is lots of soup? But no – a bowl of hot soup is really only comforting when the weather's cold, which it isn't in the Middle East. Hmm, keep exploring ...

Now I've imagined all of that – I don't know what went through Mr de Bono's mind. I'm just saying he could have used the random word method to aid his lateral thinking.

Because what I do know is that he certainly did, as an answer, suggest *Marmite*.

His reason for deciding that Marmite would reduce tensions in the Middle East? Because there they eat a lot of unleavened bread. Unleavened bread is low in zinc. And a zinc deficiency makes men irritable. Whereas Marmite is rich in zinc. Give that to men in the Middle East and they'd be a lot less tetchy ... and a lot nicer to each other.

So Marmite was the idea he presented to the Foreign Office to help bring about – as one newspaper described it – 'Peace in the Middle Yeast'.

And that's the power of being random.

Summary

Random insertion is a useful tool when you want a very different answer; a solution far from iterative and which is unlikely to be arrived at with any other kind of problem solving.

It's just as useful for innovating as it is for problem solving, because your brain can create a link between the current situation and your random trigger to create something new and innovative that may (may) have a useful benefit or advantage.

It's often not easy so you may not want to try it as the first tool with an inexperienced group. However it is useful if you or anyone else has seen something interesting or stimulating elsewhere (such as an entertaining YouTube clip) that gets people excited, which you can then ask them to somehow connect to your problem/ opportunity.

To use *random insertion* successfully, ask:

- Do we want to break out of our patterns of thinking, simply and quickly?

- Can we find a link between where we are and this random element?

- What's the bridging idea for the random element, to spark relevant ideas?

- Can we use this random object/idea to achieve a solution/ innovation?

- What have we seen that we thought was really interesting/ exciting/powerful? How could we incorporate what's good about it to achieve a solution/innovation?

X.

Interrogate and extrapolate

'If I had an hour to solve a problem I'd spend 55 minutes thinking about the problem and five minutes thinking about solutions.' ALBERT EINSTEIN

This tool can feel quite different to the others. While many of the others are about dusting off the creative part of your brain, this one can feel more logical and analytical. Which is why some people will love it and others will hate it (I'm back to Marmite again).

It's also why it won't work with every problem. But I've included it because it would be remiss not to acknowledge that some problems *can* be solved with rigorous, rational analysis.

Your car engine has broken down: where *sidestep the issue* would have you cycle or get a taxi instead, *interrogate and extrapolate* is about taking the engine apart, examining every cog and cable, finding what's wrong and putting it right.

Visual

Analytical problem solving is often like (1) – it doesn't look widely enough or deeply enough (breaking the parts into smaller elements) so the discrete nub of the issue gets missed. Only by examining every possible area, in the greatest possible detail (2), will you discover the very specific, very manageable problem (A) that needs to be solved for everything else to work.

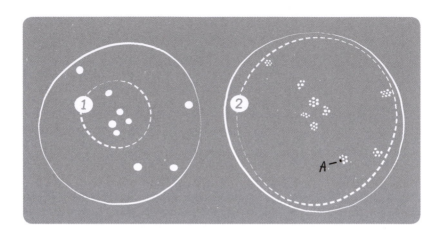

Theory

The start of this *Innovation* section was *think bigger*, taking a step (or several steps, or a leap) back from the original problem.

This tool kind of goes the other way – breaking the problem down into small, manageable pieces and discovering (perhaps) that of those pieces, the problem only resides in one or two of them – so you only need to fix those broken pieces to solve the issue.

How come both tools are valid? Well, the nature of business problems varies wildly. And a few of those problems suit a methodical approach more than a creative one. You might think of it as the difference between something that's objective and something that's subjective. When it's an objective, tangible and clearly quantifiable issue, this interrogative approach can be effective.

Seeing red

For instance, I was doing a press pass at a big printing company and we were talking about colour reproduction and checking colour accuracy. The director told me about a problem they'd had a while back when all of their work was coming out too red.

Now with modern printers (where just one press can cost £3,000,000), colour accuracy is exemplary. And expected. So it's a whacking great problem if you, the major printer, are suddenly producing work that's too red. Especially when you don't know why. Is it the inks? The paper stock? The press computers? The guys operating the press? Too much ink? Too little? The way it's drying? A problem with the varnish?

In the end, by going through every step of the process and examining them individually, they discovered the problem was . . . meat lamps.

Let me explain. Printers use viewing booths with special lighting so they can check colours accurately by eye. Your normal office strip lights just aren't clean enough. Supermarkets use special lighting too, in their meat refrigerators. Lights that emit a lot of red. To make the meat seem . . . redder. Meatier. The tricksters.

And by mistake somebody had fitted the print viewing booth with those meat lamps. So the work was printing fine. But when they looked at it in their special booth designed to show the work most accurately, the red lights meant they were seeing it the least accurately.

A simple mistake. But one that had people seriously worried. And which could have been very costly.

Now, that problem could have been solved in a number of ways, I'm sure. But it seems to me that they did it the most sensible way: they went through every stage step-by-step and found that there was a genuine, rational issue (the wrong bulbs), which they then swapped for the right ones.

So if we're going to be simplistic about it, this tool is a bit more left brain than some of the others. And by trialling both left-brain and right-brain approaches, you'll get a wider range of solutions to choose between.

Action

> **INTERROGATE AND EXTRAPOLATE TOOLKIT**
>
> 1. Break the problem down into its constituent parts, smaller and smaller, more and more specific.
>
> 2. Now establish which of those much smaller parts contain the problem and which are adequate (or even successful) as they are.
>
> 3. Finally, extrapolate out: magnify those problematic elements. Are they faults you can fix in the same methodical, logical way you used to find them? Or do you now need to use another problem-solving tool on them?

Unless you're really convinced that this tool is the one most likely to work, then I wouldn't recommend starting with it. Because it's the more logical approach, it could steer the group down very logical, rational tracks, which may make some of the other tools feel unnatural and difficult to work with afterwards.

But when you do use this tool, it has three simple and appropriately logical steps.

The first two steps

Break the problem down. Discuss it, examine it and write it out in a detailed step-by-step manner. Perhaps there's someone in the group who is particularly good at teasing through the detail who could lead this action.

Then, interrogate each of those individual parts. Study them, discuss them, understand them and break them down further if needs be.

Now it should be clear which elements hold the issues. It might just be a tiny detail of the process, a small aspect of an individual, a discrete advantage held by the competition.

The problem now feels more manageable. It's not a big problem like, 'The competition has a much better product', it's 'The competition has a product which has these three features ours doesn't have, features which appeal most to people aged 50–65'.

That kind of detail you only get from rigorous interrogation and it can be critical to how you solve the problem.

In the case I've just mentioned, you know just to add those three features. Or stop marketing to 50–65-year-olds. Or think of a new feature that appeals to 50–65-year-olds more than those three features would.

Of course, traditional problem-solving models might *start* with an approach like *interrogate and extrapolate*: really studying every contributing element of the problem and analysing it. The issue I have with that is that you can quickly lose the holistic 'let's solve the big issue in one staggeringly impactful way' view, because considering the problem in small pieces can encourage you to just tinker. It also takes up a lot of early energy and effort. That's why I recommend you use the interrogative approach as a tool in its own right, rather than as an obligatory part of the set-up.

PROBLEM-SOLVING TIP

A 'spider diagram' (for a visual, look it up on the web . . . pardon the pun) can be a great way to explore a problem and break it down into components. At the centre you draw a circle containing the whole problem. Then, as you break it up, each part becomes a new circle (or *node*) off that centre one. As you break each of those parts into smaller elements, those become new nodes branching off the part they stem from; an ever-growing diagram of smaller and smaller pieces as you move away from the centre. If there's a link between different nodes, you can draw a line to connect them.

The final step

Once you've interrogated the problem and identified the specific issue – the faulty parts, if you like – extrapolate the solution. In other words, discuss the fix, mentally put it in place and run through the scenario again, checking that having corrected those smaller issues, the whole thing works and the problem's solved. It's rather like the zany, evergreen board game *Mouse Trap*, if you know that. You fix the position of the diver so that when the marble hits the board he leaps up and lands in the tub rather than just missing it ... and suddenly the whole operation works smoothly from start to finish. You trap the mouse and win the game.

Using this tool in a group session, with a mix of people who have different insights, levels of experience and a range of skills, can be really useful. You're discussing the aspects of the problem in detail, and by breaking it down into discrete elements everyone can understand, an 'outsider' can come up with a way of fixing that one little cog that will get the whole machine working again.

Example

You're on the motorway and there's a sign. There's been an accident and the middle and outside lanes of the road are going to close, 800 metres ahead.

So what do you do?

In England, you do one of two things. You either move into the slow lane straight away, becoming part of a huge, single-file queue.

Or you're one of those self-centred, sociopathic so-and-sos who speeds down the empty lanes, past the long line of (impatiently) queuing traffic, then tries to force their way in at the last minute. Which the people who've been queuing in the slow lane don't like, so they squeeze up, bumper to bumper to try and keep you out, increasing their risk of having a prang.

It's stressful for both types of driver, and it's a potential source of accidents.

Zip it

If you interrogate the flow of traffic, the data, the simple fact that while there are three lanes open it seems odd to have most of the traffic create an extra-long queue in one of them . . . you'd realise that there was a better way. That way being the *late merge* (or 'zipper' system), as used (by law) in countries like Germany and Austria.

There, you're expected to keep using all the lanes. Instead of being frowned on for not joining the slow lane a.s.a.p., you stay where you are. Then, when you get to the point where the road actually closes, everybody adopts a 'zipper' approach. So if you're in the slow lane, you let one car in the middle lane filter in. Then you go. Then the car behind you lets one in. And so on. Like a zip.

In fact, the zipper system doesn't mean more cars get past the road closure in any given time – it doesn't increase 'throughput'. But it does reduce the length of the queue (it's shorter because it's wider) and it does reduce the difference in speed between the different lanes, which increases safety. And you'd imagine it reduces the stress levels of everyone involved too. Those in the slow lane don't feel that cars in the other lanes are jumping the queue, while people in the other lanes don't have to fret about trying to squeeze their way in, because they know they'll be let in, like the alternating teeth of a zip.

> **PROBLEM-SOLVING TIP**
>
> You can also try making things worse. Take the problem you have and ask: what would make it a bigger problem? Exaggerate the issue, worsen the situation, downgrade the product/service. The group will relish this activity. Once you've done it, pause and then *reverse* the actions people suggested – and you may come up with new ways to lessen the problem. Strangely, people may find it easier to exaggerate a problem first, before they work out how to achieve the opposite.

Several tools in this book might have helped develop the same zipper solution. But *interrogate and extrapolate* would seem to be a good bet for it. It's a logical problem, a matter of maths and physics – finding a way to maximise the available space on the road while creating a simple and fair system for drivers to deal with the obstacle.

It can work really well for you too. Just, as I say, don't turn to it first every time, or you may find you get bogged down in too much detail too early. Because, to offer a conflicting point of view, as Malcolm Forbes (publisher of *Forbes* magazine) posits, 'It's so much easier to suggest solutions when you don't know too much about the problem.'

Summary

Interrogate and extrapolate is generally more useful for solving problems than capitalising on opportunities. If you use it for innovating, it's likely to give you incremental improvements rather than transformative ones.

It's particular useful for problems that seem rational and where you have a lot of information and detail (since you can't interrogate them if you aren't able to find out lots and lots about them). Where there are lots of unknowns or things are vague or nebulous, you probably wouldn't choose this tool first.

In fact, this tool is also often the tool we automatically use when confronted with a problem – but often rather half-heartedly. People just use the information they already have or know, or just do easy, lazy research.

So, to use *interrogate and extrapolate* successfully, ask:

- Are we being a modern-day Sherlock Holmes, gathering as much data as possible and analysing and understanding and debating everything we possibly can about it?

- Are we drilling down into enough detail? Are we breaking every part into its constituent parts, smaller and smaller, perhaps with a spider diagram?

- Can we find the real nub of the problem – the small part of parts which were hiding within the whole – and solve that, in a similarly logical, analytical way? Or do we now need another tool to solve it?

xi.
Solve something simpler

'Simplicity is the ultimate sophistication.'
LEONARDO DA VINCI

In business we're always being told to raise our sights. To aim higher. To achieve more. To go further.

But what if – sometimes – we don't set our sights so high? What if – occasionally – we settle for second best? What if – once in a while – we achieve a bit less? Do 'just enough' and no more?

It's a bit like the Pareto Principle – the 80/20 rule. It may be that solving a simpler problem, with a cheaper, quicker, easier solution (one that requires just 20 per cent of the effort) still gives us 80 per cent of the advantage. And 80 per cent is a pretty good score. At school, 80 per cent is usually an A. At university, it's a First. And in business, it might be enough to get the job done.

So solving something simpler is about first asking, 'Do we really *have* to solve this problem? Let's not ignore it completely … but let's look at something a bit easier that might get us near enough to where we want to be.'

Visual

The apocryphal story is that because an ordinary pen wouldn't work in space, NASA spent 10 years and $10 million developing the Space Pen. But if you state the right issue, 'We just need something to make notes with in space', you get what the USSR's cosmonauts were given instead. A pencil.

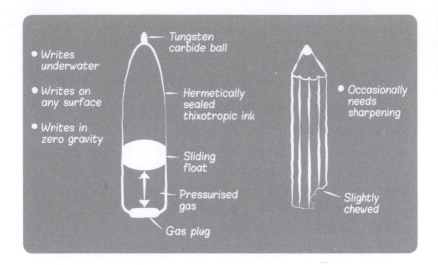

- Writes underwater
- Writes on any surface
- Writes in zero gravity

Tungsten carbide ball

Hermetically sealed thixotropic ink

Sliding float

Pressurised gas

Gas plug

- Occasionally needs sharpening

Slightly chewed

Theory

Make the problem simpler and often, of course, the solution will be too.

We've all heard the term 'over-engineered'. Where someone's gone much further than they needed to in solving a problem or meeting a challenge. Either to the point where it becomes detrimental, or where it's just needlessly complex or expensive or demanding.

The Contrarotator, for example, Dyson's purple washing machine. It was brilliantly made. Even the ball bearings were aircraft grade apparently (whatever that means). But all that engineering excellence came at a price: twice the price, in fact, of other washing machines. Three times the price of some.

And it was better than people needed (or were prepared to pay for). So despite being really good, the sales were really bad. And Dyson had to abandon it.

Try being lazy

Solve something simpler is like the opposite of over-engineering: instead of looking for the best possible solution to the problem, you just look for a simpler, lazier version of the problem. And once you've got that, you can come up with a 'cheat' solution: you're solving a problem which looks, in many ways, like the original problem, but which is much easier to achieve.

You might think of it as putting a Band-Aid on the problem – but that's not necessarily a disparaging term, as Malcolm Gladwell points out in his bestselling book *The Tipping Point*: 'The Band-Aid is an inexpensive, convenient and remarkably versatile solution to an astonishing array of problems. In their history, Band-Aids have probably allowed millions of people to keep working or playing tennis or cooking or walking when they would otherwise have had to stop. The Band-Aid solution is actually the best kind of solution because it involves solving a problem with the minimum amount of effort and time and cost.'

The good news is, our brains do this all the time anyway. Because many decisions have more variables than we can hold in our head at any one time, our brains cheat. They fall into habits of substitution: they substitute a difficult problem for an easier one – look up the *effort-reduction framework* by Anuj Shah and Daniel Oppenheimer ('Heuristics Made Easy', *Psychological Bulletin* 134/2, 1998).

(Although, somewhat worryingly, we often don't realise our brain has cheated and answered an easier question than the one asked of it.)

So, as long as everyone can accept that solving the simpler problem is OK, then you're giving yourself an easier starting point – and thus more chance of getting to the finish line.

Action

SOLVE SOMETHING SIMPLER TOOLKIT

1. Do you have to solve the problem? What if you didn't? Perhaps you can just solve the consequences instead (they may be simpler to deal with).

2. Or maybe you can even just solve the challenges of living with the consequences.

3. Ask the right question to find the 'next best thing': is there part of the problem you could solve to get you close to the solution you want – perhaps by looking at the crux of the issue?

4. Or ask the right question to say, 'What could we solve instead, that's a bit easier, to get the same or a similar result?'

As you can see from the toolkit panel, there are a few ways to look at this approach. But they're always about *not* solving the problem you've got (or not wholly, anyway).

There are a couple of good commercial reasons for the *solve something simpler* tool. The first is resource – solving the problem as you're presented with it may just require an inordinate amount of time and money and effort. Back to the 80/20 rule. If you can get 80 per cent of the benefit for considerably less than 80 per cent of the cost, then that might just be commercially more sensible.

The second benefit of *solve something simpler* is that it moves the business forward when otherwise nothing may have happened. There may be a business issue or challenge that's gone unaddressed because everyone knows what the solution is, but they know it's too expensive or demanding. And so nothing gets done.

This is a way around that: a wake-up call to say, 'OK, we're not going to fully tackle the problem right now, but let's do *something* that gets us closer to where we want to be'.

You might call *solve something simpler* the 'quick fix' approach.

PROBLEM-SOLVING TIP

Research showed people were put off instant cake mix because they didn't believe you could make a decent cake just from powdered mix. Instead of solving the (difficult) problem of trying to convince people that *yes you could*, the manufacturers did something simpler. They removed the dried egg from the recipe and told customers that they needed to add their own egg to the cake mix.

Customers liked that they had to add a fresh egg; now it felt like 'lazy baking' rather than 'fake baking'. And sales went up.

The first method

Discuss the problem and examine what will happen if you *don't* solve it. Perhaps the consequences of leaving the problem to go unchecked are easier to solve than the problem itself. In effect: what if you treat the symptoms, not the cause?

It can be almost heretical to suggest, 'Hey, what if we don't bother solving the problem?', but a rational, objective analysis might identify that the problem is very difficult and resource-intensive to solve, but the consequences of it aren't. Fixing a leak might be difficult, for some reason. Sticking a bucket under the leak and emptying it every once in a while probably isn't.

The second method

Here, you don't solve the problem *and* you don't solve the consequences of the problem. You just solve the way things work when you're living with the consequences of the problem, so they're no longer an issue. You negate them as much as you can.

Another simple home example: say your neighbour has a tree with branches that overhang your garden. You don't mind the branches, but it means that part of your garden is in permanent shade and the grass won't grow there. You could trim the branches that overhang your side, that's your legal right. But it's going to be a fair bit of work and need doing regularly. Or you could ask your neighbour to cut the tree down. Maybe he says yes – as long as you pay for it.

Or perhaps you could just adapt to the consequences: solve the challenges of living *with* the problem. So you create a neat border around the area where the grass won't grow and you plant it with bluebells that thrive happily under the shade of a tree.

> **PROBLEM-SOLVING TIP**
>
> With this tool you've got to work hard to 'ask the right question'. A simple, elegant expression of what the biggest issue with this problem is will really help people find simple, 'good enough' solutions. So spend time asking different questions of the problem, get different people to be provocative with it and ask awkward questions until you get something that you think you can find a quick fix for. If you can, and you realise that quick fix will make a significant difference relatively easily, then you should seriously consider it.

The third method

Take the problem apart and find the crux of the issue (like with *interrogate and extrapolate*). Ask, 'What's the *problem within the problem*?' It may be that you just want to achieve (or remove) an effect related to the crux – which can be much simpler to do. Unlike *interrogate and extrapolate,* you're still not going to correct that element fully; we're still looking for the lazy way out.

For instance, many years ago I had a car where the electric motor of one of the rear windows broke. Not only did it mean the window couldn't be opened and closed, the motor no longer gripped the window so it was just permanently gaping open. Not great security. I took it to the garage and they gave me a quote to order and fit a new electric motor. It was around £180 I think. Heck, I said – that's a lot to fix an electric window I don't really use. All I really want is the window to be secure. Isn't there anything else you can do?

Well, they said . . . we could just open up the door panel, jam in a bit of wood to hold the window closed and put the door panel back on. £40.

So that's what they did. Because I didn't need the whole problem solving. It was a rear window that was rarely used. I didn't *really* need a rear window that opened and closed with the press of a button. I just needed a window that was secure. That was the next best thing. And a simpler, quicker, cheaper problem to solve.

In every case, what you'll need in your brainstorm session is some commercial awareness and pragmatism.

It's about achieving a balance: you're not going to completely address the issue, but neither are you going to ignore it.

But you've come to believe that solving the problem as it stands is impossible. Or a cost/benefit analysis has revealed solving it just isn't commercially viable. But a quick fix might make a really useful difference.

Example

For mobile phone manufacturers like Samsung, performance is an important competitive advantage. If your phone is faster and more powerful than the competition, many people will choose your product over the rival's.

Of course, always having the latest technology (preferably without charging customers more) is a constant battle and very resource-hungry. It's a significant, ongoing challenge.

But what if we can *solve something simpler*, by examining the problem and asking the right question?

So ... people want the fastest phone. Well ... how do they know what the fastest phone is?

One answer: benchmarking tests. Although most people won't know the numbers or specific results, they may hear that 'in benchmarking tests' (speed and performance tests run by independent third parties), phone A outperformed phone B.

Well, OK then. Now we've got a simpler challenge to solve. The *best* solution is to have a phone that's simply faster and more powerful in every way, all of the time. But the *next best thing* is to have a phone that's faster at a critical time: when it's being benchmarked. That's the crux of the problem.

And by 'lowering our sights' and being less ambitious, we've got something more achievable.

So what's a simple way for Samsung to ensure its phones get the best possible benchmarking score? By (allegedly) adding a bit of code to their phone's OS that recognises when a benchmark is being run. And when it does, it raises the thermal limits (allowing the phone to get hotter than normal), as well as the GPU frequency and CPU voltage/frequency, to get the highest benchmarking score.

In other words, the phone goes into a short-term, unsustainable 'turbo' mode when it knows it's being benchmarked, to get an artificially high score.

Because adding that bit of code to your OS is a much simpler problem to solve than always having a faster, more advanced CPU than your competitor's.

But it still gives you an answer that's close to the one you want.

Summary

Solve something simpler is about finding the 'sticking plaster' answer; agreeing that it's OK not to solve the whole problem, but just do enough to reduce its effect. Generally it's a tool for problem solving not opportunity seizing, but it can be handy at simplifying the opportunity too, to give you something easier to reach for and attain.

To use *solve something simpler* successfully, ask:

- Can we agree that solving the problem in its entirety is going to require too many resources or is simply impractical?

- What if we just solve the symptoms, not the cause?

- Or what if we don't solve even the symptoms, but find a way to live with them/negate them?

- Or, what's a simpler, more modest version of the problem? If we solved this easier problem, would we get a reasonable result?

- What's 'the right question' we need to ask – what's the problem within the problem that might be enough to solve. Like with my broken electric window, instead of solving the cause (difficult/expensive), can we just solve the effect (easy/cheap)?

xii.
Combine and redefine

'Innovation makes the world go round. It brings prosperity and freedom.' ROBERT METCALFE

Not everything can be successfully combined. But when it comes to cracking a tough problem, or trying to jimmy open a clamped-shut opportunity, using a range of tools can really help.

Which means employing several tools one after another, to see how they augment the initial solution or how they give you an A, an A+B and an A+B+C solution to choose between.

I would always suggest using more than one tool anyway, to see which gives you the best answer. This *Combine* theory just acknowledges that sometimes using multiple tools can create a unique answer, because the thinking you get from running your third tool has been influenced by the thinking and idea generation you've already done from running the first two tools.

Visual

Build on your progress: here the first tool used comes up with five possible first-stage solutions (1), some of which can be pushed to the second or third stage. But taking one of those second-stage ideas and developing it with a second tool moves it on to a couple of stage-four ideas. Using a third creative thinking tool on one of those gets us to the fifth stage (5), which in this example achieves the goal: a workable implementable solution to the problem.

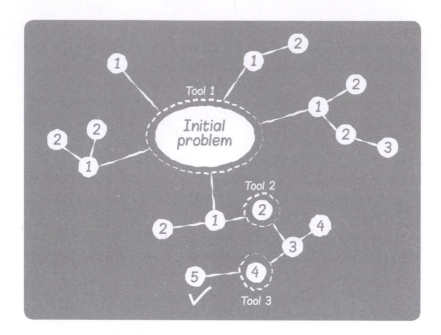

Theory

If you've ever seen *House*, about an American diagnostician played by Hugh Laurie, you'll see, in episode after episode, something will happen that gives him the lightbulb moment where he diagnoses the patient's incredibly rare and esoteric condition. Something someone says (apparently unrelated) or something he sees (apparently unrelated) triggers a memory, makes him realise something or causes him to make a connection ... he pauses, stares into the middle distance ... and *ping*, his eyes light up. He's cracked it.

But in real life it's rarely like that. In real life, it can be hard to pinpoint what it was that gave you that lightbulb moment, your 'flash of inspiration'.

And so it is here. Using several tools gives you more cracks at the nut – it might be the third tool you use that gives you the best solution, but perhaps only because you tried another two tools first, which moved things along enough for the third one to deliver the killer blow.

In other words, using several tools one after another can create a transient, hybrid tool – a kind of '*thinking bigger* to *solve something simpler* with a *constraint* that involves *choice architecture*' tool, for instance.

And that sounds like a very rare kind of breakthrough.

Action

COMBINE AND REDEFINE TOOLKIT

1. Choose a creative thinking tool you want to use to address the problem/opportunity/innovation need.

2. Have the 11 individual tools in mind at all times; it may be that a particular tool seems particularly well suited to building on the progress you've made with a prior tool.

3. After you've used one tool, instead of going back to the original issue and starting again with a new tool (which is what you've been doing previously), this time look at the progress you've made and continue from that point, to take it further, by employing a second or third tool.

Using this final tool is very simple – it's about combining multiples of the previous 11.

In any brainstorming session – whether you're solving a problem, capitalising on an opportunity or searching for an innovation – you'll use several tools, not just one.

But that's tackling the same problem with different tools, whereas *combine and redefine* is about using a sequence of tools to build upon each other. Using one tool takes you so far, using another tool takes that progress a bit further, using a third tool gets you over the finish line.

So, in your session you run one tool (tool A) on the problem. It doesn't feel like you've got a great solution, so you try tool B on the same problem, at the same starting point. Again, it doesn't feel like you've cracked it, so you try tool C.

That gives you a breakthrough – a good result.

Taking things further

Now review the whole suite of tools and choose another tool to work with. Perhaps in this case someone thinks that going back to tool A and using it on the current solution you have (as a result of using tool C) could take things further (*cracking*). And after that, someone has an idea that using tool D will make the solution even stronger still, or add a useful new advantage (*stacking*).

Play with the arrangement

It may be that choosing three tools and using them in a different order would give a different result, and that may concern your group – how do they choose the 'best' order to run the tools in, so they can iteratively build on success?

In truth there's probably no way of knowing in advance. Just experiment, play with it and try running different tools in different orders. But as I say, you'll often find that after running one tool someone gets a feel for what next tool would dovetail effectively with it.

Finally, there's a bonus half-tool I'll squeeze in here because it's about *redefining* how you approach problem solving. I call it the *equivalence approach*.

This means looking at how someone else (in an unrelated field, preferably) has solved a problem – not the same problem you have, but perhaps one that has a little overlap or commonality. So you know *what* they did, now you brainstorm ideas around *how* they might have come up with their solution/innovation. You might not be right, of course, but you may still come up with a post-rationalised method you could use yourself. You'll have created your own brand new problem-solving tool. And if you do, please let me know and (with your permission) maybe I'll include it in the next edition of this book.

It's not quite the same as *think like another*, which means having the mindset of another person or brand; it just means asking a question like, 'How did Barclays come up with their Ping-it app, which gets around the problem of being able to send money securely via a mobile, even if you're not a Barclays customer?'

So there you are – 12.5 tools for the price of 12.

Example

Dyson is a client I've worked with; a fantastic example of a man, company and brand that has dared to solve problems differently and achieved great success as a result.

I remember having a meeting in a board room at Dyson with a large glass table that James Dyson had designed. Not a conventional glass table, mind; this one didn't have any legs. Instead there were thick steel cables clamped to the ceiling that came in at an angle, through holes in the desk, then back out wide to clamps on the floor. So the glass table top floated in mid-air.

Anyway, as everyone knows, James was turned down by all the major vacuum cleaner manufacturers with his bagless invention. He had to create his own company to get it made. A company which has continued to innovate ever since.

In fact a recent TV ad for the very slim, handheld Dyson talks about how the smaller, faster digital motor was compact enough to fit in the handle. This made it better balanced and easier to use. And in the ad, presented by Mr Dyson himself, he talks of challenging conventions (tool iii: *be contrary*).

But I want to look at how Dyson has taken another problem and solved it with a *combination* of creative thinking tools to innovate a breakthrough solution.

Here's the problem: in the UK, the weather's not really hot enough for long enough for most people to invest in air conditioning at home. If it gets really hot, we might use a fan. But fans are a bit rubbish. The blades chop the air, so it feels irritating. They're also distractingly noisy and those whirling blades mean they have to have a grille to make them safe(r) for children and animals, which makes them ugly.

So let's solve that problem. First of all, let's give ourselves a constraint (tool iv: *be constrained*). And the constraint is: develop a fan that has no blades. It's never been done before. There are thousands upon thousands of fans out there by hundreds of different manufacturers, and they all have blades. So let's insist that whatever we come up with, it has to be blade-free.

Hmm ... The Dyson engineers go away and work out how you can make air move without blades. They come back with an idea reminiscent of a jet engine, drawing in up to 33 litres of air per second. Suddenly you've got a fan that you feel safer using when children are around, because they can't stick their fingers/tongue/a knife through the grille to hit the blades. In fact, we don't even need the grille any more.

But let's go further with our redesign. We've got a fan without blades, so we're solving the problem of the whirring noise, of the dangers if it tips over and even maybe the problem of the buffeting, chopped air. But can we do more? What if we *think like another* (tool ii).

So how about Apple? Because, believe me, many people at Dyson consider their brand to be the Apple of the markets they're in. So how would Apple make a fan? It would be beautiful, sculptural, elegant ... and so perfectly balanced you could tilt it to any angle with just one finger.

And instead of having three or four fixed power settings, you'd have a single dial (without any clumsy wording written by it, obviously) so you could change the power of the fan to precisely the level that suited you.

And if you look at the Dyson Air Multiplier, that's exactly what you'll find. A beautiful, sculptural, minimalist, blade-free fan using (hidden) innovative technology.

Solving one problem, creating another

However, we have created a new problem. All that development time … was expensive.

So our fandangled spandangled new fan is going to have to be pretty pricey. (Currently the Dyson desktop fan is about seven times the price of a cheap one with blades.)

Now this is a problem I don't think Dyson has solved – at the time of writing, it seems to me they've simply ignored it. Of course, over time the price may come down as the cost of manufacturing falls and they cover their development costs. And they market it as the best fan there is, so if you've got pots of money and you want the best, then you'll buy it.

But I think they could go further: perhaps by using *sidestep the issue* (tool viii). Instead of ignoring the problem, how could they sidestep it the way Stella Artois did for their high price?

Perhaps they could position the Dyson Air Multiplier as more than simply a fan, but also as a piece of art for your desk or room or office. Because it might be expensive for a fan, but it's cheap for a modern sculpture. Imagine doing some product placement in films and TV programmes, the way every laptop user in the movies has an Apple. A beautiful piece of sculpture in the living room of a Jennifer Lawrence film: Dyson fans would quickly get many more … fans (sorry).

Or could they *solve something simpler* (tool xi). Instead of trying to find ways to reduce the price (which might be a valid but challenging route), could they just make it seem better value? For instance, they offer a five-year guarantee on their vacuums, but only a two-year guarantee on their fans. Why's that?

The price of a Dyson vacuum is not seven times the price of a cheap vacuum, unlike the fan price disparity. So they should at least match the guarantee – perhaps double it. (After all, for most people in the UK, the fan's not going to get *that* much use, so you'd hope it would last 10 years.) And if you advertised the product with a 10-year guarantee then the price wouldn't seem so steep, because you knew the fan was going to last. In fact, customers might divide the price by 10 in their heads and think, 'Oh, per year that's pretty good value.'

Perhaps they could *think like another* (tool ii). Furniture stores like DFS, for example – they're always advertising their 'buy now, pay later' schemes. 'Pay nothing for a year then pay 12 interest-free instalments of just £XX' for example. There's no reason Dyson couldn't do that; a two-year payment period would be no longer than the guarantee they're currently offering anyway.

We could go on, but I think the point's been made. Dyson, it might be suggested, has created a breakthrough product using a combination of problem-solving/innovation tools. And by exploring a few more tools, you can see how we could take things further still.

Summary

Combine and redefine is not about just using one tool after another (which you'll do anyway), but about seeing if one tool can build on the progress made by a previous one. You'll need to experiment to see what the 'best' order of tools is for your particular challenge.

It can be just as effective for capitalising on an opportunity/ developing an innovation as it is for problem solving. And it's best used when you're talking about a significant problem or opportunity and you have the time you need to explore it fully.

It's also one you'll get better at over time – make a little progress with one tool and instinctively you'll get a feel for which other tool will help you move things on further. You'll create favourite combinations from individual tools, like coming up with a pleasing chord from individual notes.

To use *combine and redefine* successfully, ask:

- Can we *stack* the benefits with more than one tool (as in the Dyson example), or use multiple tools to *crack* the problem further?
- Are we persevering with one tool for long enough?
- But are we alert to when another tool is itching to jump in?

PART III
INSPIRATION

'It isn't that they can't see the solution. It is that they can't see the problem.' GILBERT K. CHESTERTON

Now you've got the tools you need. But how will you put them into practice? In Part III we'll look at how to run your sessions to give yourself the best chance of success. We'll also explore how to get your ideas implemented.

After all, how many times have you been part of a great brainstorm but:

- you've known in your heart of hearts that nothing was going to come of it;

- you've believed any bold ideas you came up with were going to be diluted beyond recognition before they got implemented;

- you've looked back a few days later at what you came up with and actually been a bit disappointed, because it wasn't as strong as you'd remembered?

And, perhaps most common of all, how many times have you been in a brainstorm and it's given you a headache rather than a headrush?

To run a strong session, there are four key areas we should explore:

1. Preparation

2. Generation

3. Development

4. Implementation

I'll look at these four areas while making a big assumption: that you're running a group session.

That may not always be the case of course; you may want (or need) to crack a problem/find an opportunity by yourself. Or with just one other person. And you might be sitting on the sofa or at a desk or in the car rather than in a gleaming, well-appointed board room (or other, more stimulating environment).

And that's absolutely fine. When you find yourself with an available hour or so and you decide to look at a troubling issue, or start exploring an opportunity, really all you need to get going are the creative thinking tools in Part II. There are, of course, plenty of examples throughout history of one person working alone and thinking up something quite wonderful without the need for colleagues or a flipchart.

What's more, in the *Preparation* section that follows, I'll explain why some individual brainstorming is vital even as part of a group session.

But, when it's a big business issue with potentially significant gains, you will – usually – benefit from putting together a group of people. In the right room. With the right timeframe to hatch and nurture your breakthroughs.

1.
Preparation

'Doing what's right isn't the problem. It's knowing what's right.' LYNDON B. JOHNSON

I'm not going to labour the point here; it's all simple stuff but it's also an area where some problem-solving models get bogged down.

To *prepare* for your brainstorming session, think about these five things:

First, invite the right people. People relevant to the problem area. Perhaps people who, in some way, are causing the problem. People who are probably going to be involved in the solution's implementation. People you think are creative thinkers. People who have no connection with the problem, and therefore bring fewer preconceptions in with them. And decision makers in the relevant area. You may not be agreeing a way forward there and then, but it's very, very good practice to have people in the room who are later able to green light your solution.

> **PROBLEM-SOLVING TIP**
>
> 'Radical innovations often happen at the intersections of disciplines,' write Dr Karim Lakhani and Dr Lars Bo Jeppesen in the *Harvard Business Review* of May 2007 ('Getting unusual suspects to solve R&D puzzles'). 'The more diverse the problem-solving population, the more likely a problem is to be solved. People tend to link problems that are distant from their fields with solutions that they've encountered in their own work.' Make sure you've got people from different areas in the session, to create your own cross-departmental supergroup.

Second, spend some time studying the problem so you have a good understanding of it – its history, how significant it is, which people and areas it affects. If you can monetise it – e.g. get an estimate of how much it might be costing the business – then you're giving everyone in the session a great incentive to fix it.

Your research might give you some good material for helping solve the problem (or capitalise on the opportunity, if that's the purpose of the session you're having) and it will certainly be good for giving everyone a 'potted history/state of the nation' address so everyone has the same understanding. Partly for the people you're inviting along who might not be very close to the problem, but partly because you'll often find people close to the issue still have different understandings – or different versions – of the truth.

Ensuring everyone has the same, objective and factual understanding of the problem can get you halfway there. 'A problem well stated is a problem half-solved,' as inventor Charles Kettering said.

Third: props. Some of the creative-thinking tools suit having props anyway (such as *think like another*), but there may be other things you want to bring along. Ideally, you'll hold the session somewhere different to the norm – maybe you can borrow the function room of a local pub or bar; perhaps there's a museum or gallery or local attraction that has a room available. A different venue can be really stimulating. But, if you have to do it in one of your usual meeting rooms, props will help the session feel different from a typical meeting.

Things like magazines (useful for the icebreaker idea that follows), amusing YouTube videos to get everyone in a positive mood, crayons or chalks instead of pens, modelling clay, board games, interesting objects – anything you reckon might help people free up their minds and develop their thinking, as well as make the session more stimulating and memorable.

Fourth: have the problem written out nice and big, to stick up for everyone to refer to throughout (not just on the first page of the flipchart, vanishing from sight as soon as you start collecting ideas). Having the problem visible at all times will help keep everyone on brief, looking at a standardised expression of the problem, not the version of it they keep in their own head.

And finally, make sure you've got the basic stuff you need for a brainstorm – flipchart, paper, pens, sticky notes or cards, sweets/cakes (a bit of sugar has, I believe, been shown to give your thinking a short-term boost), a good-sized room ... and enough time booked with everyone for the session to be meaningful. A whole morning, generally. Which is where monetising the problem/opportunity comes in useful. If people are saying they can only spare an hour, remind them there's £2 million (or whatever the figure is) at stake. Wouldn't they like to be the person who saved/made the company two million quid in a morning?

(The truth is you may well need more than one session, and you might certainly hold a second session to develop the ideas you've generated. But after your spectacularly successful first brainstorm, getting people back together for subsequent *ideation* should be much easier.)

OK, that's your pre-session prep sorted: you're ready with a boxful of iced doughnuts, blank postcards, felt-tips, old magazines and video clips of cats playing the piano. But there's also some in-session prep: briefing the team on how you're going to run things and their role in the session.

Structure for the session

At the start of your brainstorm, go through this six-point plan with people on how you're going to run things.

i. **Immersion**: You'll state the problem, give its history, background, context and whatever else is relevant – and check everyone's understanding.

ii. **Movie**: You'll split into sub-groups to create a film poster of the problem (optional icebreaker, see below).

iii. **TOM**: Everyone will capture their Top-Of-Mind ideas for solving the problem (see below).

iv. **Tool**: Then you'll explain the creative thinking tool to use.

v. **1M1**: The session then takes a one-many-one brainstorming format (see below).

(Steps iv and v are repeated several times with different tools.)

vi. **Vote**: As a group, you select the 'best' ideas to re-look at in a future development session.

Of course there's no problem-solving law (not that anyone's told me about anyway). So if there are any of these steps you want to miss out or do differently, then just do what feels right for you and your brainstorming supergroup.

TOM

Everyone should get a few minutes to individually capture any 'Top-Of-Mind' ideas they've had just from hearing the problem (or which they'd had previously, having already known about the problem). Otherwise they may get frustrated that they've got an idea but it doesn't fit with the tool you're currently running. So they won't concentrate properly or participate fully. They might even forget the idea they had – and you might possibly, maybe, perhaps have lost a little gem.

So give everyone a chance to write down their initial ideas first – you can then collect them and write them up on the flipchart while everyone is having their first individual brainstorm using the first creative thinking tool you've chosen.

1M1

That just means 'one-many-one' – i.e. people brainstorm individually, then together as a group, then again individually. Why? Because group brainstorms can encourage some people but discourage others, depending on their personality. They can also set everyone's thinking in too-similar a direction, following the format of the first few ideas generated. And, if you run a group-only session, you're actually likely to get fewer ideas in total. Plus, a bit of individual quiet time can help people focus their thinking.

All reasons why it's better to start by getting everyone to work on individual ideas and contribute them to the flipchart. *Then* brainstorm as a group. You'll find some of the individual ideas on the flipchart trigger new ideas from the group. By discussing the ideas already generated, people's brains will become fired up and generate even more ideas.

Then, afterwards, give people the chance to take the ideas they like best and build on them, or come up with new individual ideas, fired up by the group session, before reporting back again. Let everyone know this time they can work in mini groups of two or three if they'd prefer that to working individually.

I can't tell you what a difference the 1M1 approach makes – just try it and see. Combining the best of individual and group brainstorming like this should take you much further than either would alone.

> **PROBLEM-SOLVING TIP**
>
> 'Good is a good start.' Very often, great ideas come about by building on good ideas – so one person has a good idea which gives someone else a new idea which someone else then adds to and so on (read *How Breakthroughs Happen* by Andrew Hargadon). So create an environment where ideas can be generated and also added to. Let one idea spark another, spark another, spark another, spark the winner.

You can also invoke the 'classic rules' of brainstorming. There's a visual for them in the next section, but they're listed below, based on the original four rules of Alex Osborn's 1953 *Applied Imagination* (where the term brainstorming was first popularised). I'm sure you've seen them oodles of times before, but they are worth reiterating at the start of a session as, although people know them, they still often forget them in the heat of the moment.

Rules for the session

i.   Quantity – Just get lots of ideas down.

ii. Acceptance – No judgements or criticism at this generation stage.

iii. Welcome unusual ideas (it's easier to later pour water on a fiery idea than oil on a barely flickering one).

iv. Combine – Add to and build upon ideas (without debating them at great length).

v.   Don't talk over one another.

vi. Make sure ideas are accurately captured.

Finally, as mentioned in the six-point session structure, you may want to run an icebreaker event before you give the group a tool to crack the problem with. Just to get everyone warmed up, interacting, contributing and creative.

A good icebreaker is to divide the group into smaller teams (say 12 people become three teams of four) and get them to create a poster. Using pens, flipchart paper and magazines, scissors and glue, can they create a film poster which brings the problem/ opportunity to life? They could do it as a horror, a thriller, a comedy, a rom-com, a period drama, an action movie – whatever they want. (If you want, you could assign each group a different movie genre to get different takes on the same challenge/opportunity.)

Give each group 15 minutes to create their film poster, plus a minute to present back their idea to everyone. It's a good way to get everyone discussing the problem in a fun and stimulating exercise before you move on to *generation*. Stick the movie posters up next to the matter-of-fact version of the problem you've got written out and you're ready for the ideation magic.

2.
Generation

'A mind, once stretched by a new idea, never regains its original dimensions.' OLIVER WENDELL HOLMES

You think coming up with new ideas and brilliant solutions is tough? So is effectively running a brainstorming session. And both the facilitator and participants might need several sessions until everyone clicks with the approach – especially here, where they'll be using new, creative thinking tools for the first time.

Just getting the hang of any given tool and establishing the best way to run a brainstorming session can take a bit of persistence, practice and training – before you even get to the problem you want to solve or opportunity you want to maximise.

Demonstrate ESP

If you're the facilitator an important skill to show is ESP: *encourage, support, provoke. Encourage* people in the group: get them fired up and enthused about contributing. *Support* their ideas – help the group debate them and develop them and help them turn a tiny seed of an idea into a flourishing solution. And *provoke*: when the group is becoming staid or the ideas are getting a bit flat, be ready to throw in a controversial idea or challenge people a little more. You need to be creating energy, then harnessing and directing that energy.

Over time a group will start to middle out at a level it finds comfortable – especially if individuals are starting to get a bit tired. That's why (after a triple-espresso coffee break) you've got to fire them up again and get them hitting those peaks 'out of their comfort zone'.

Structure for the session	Rules for the session
i. Immersion	● **Quantity** Just get lots of ideas down
ii. Movie	● **Acceptance** No judgements or criticism at this stage
iii. Top-Of-Mind	● **Welcome unusual ideas**
iv. Creative-thinking tool	● **Combine** Add to/build upon ideas (without lengthy debate)
v. 1M1 (One-Many-One)	
vi. Vote	● **Don't talk over one another**
Steps iv. and v. are repeated *using a different tool each time.*	● **Make sure ideas are** **accurately captured**

So you've been through the session structure and the rules of brainstorming, and you've outlined (and stuck up) the problem/opportunity/innovation need. You may have also run the movie poster icebreaker. And you'll have asked people to write down their Top-Of-Mind ideas.

Now you'll go through the creative thinking tool with the group, using the visual and the details described in the *action* part of the tool's explanation.

It's up to you which problem-solving tools you choose to introduce, and when. Typically, for an initial session I'd suggest that you try two different tools for 40 minutes each, then give everyone a 10-minute break, then use another two tools for 40 minutes each. Then you might choose to have a mini-development session (perhaps using the *combine and redefine* approach) for another 40 minutes.

PROBLEM-SOLVING TIP

Give Electronic brainstorming (EBS) a go if you can. People link up via a chat program or other peer-to-peer software, using avatars or names (e.g. Mr Red, Mr White etc. a là *Reservoir Dogs*) to make contributions anonymously. People add their ideas, which are seen instantly by everyone else connected. People can build on those ideas or use them as inspiration for their own.

There are a number of advantages of EBS: you can do it with larger numbers of people than you can fit in one meeting room; people don't have to wait for someone else to finish before having their 'turn'; people aren't influenced by *who* said the idea (because it's anonymous); and because the ideas are being typed in they're automatically captured for later analysis. It's not hard to set up so I'd recommend at least trying it, to see if it works for you.

As the session progresses, be sure that the 'rules' of brainstorming are being adhered to – particularly focusing on getting a good quantity of ideas down and not judging or criticising ideas. Keep the energy up, the mood positive and encourage people to feel as relaxed and un-selfconscious as possible.

PROBLEM-SOLVING TIP

You know who's no good in a brainstorm? Perfectionists. You can't expect every idea you come up with to be good or right or 'perfect'. So don't try – or you'll say nothing. Encourage people to say whatever pops into their head; 'verbal diarrhoea' is good in a brainstorm, providing everyone gets to speak. Aim to come up with 50 ideas rather than five. Because, as Linus Pauling said, 'The best way to have a good idea is to have a lot of ideas.'

Running your session like this means you've spent a morning gathering ideas – and you'll doubtless have a great quantity of them. Some of those ideas may be partially developed. It's possible that one or two of them have sprung out of someone's head fully-formed and flawless, like when Mozart composed whole arias without ever feeling the need to reach for the quill eraser. But a good many more of them will be seed ideas: fertile and full of potential. But in need of *development*.

Flippin' flipcharts

I say flipchart; perhaps you're capturing the outputs in a more contemporary fashion (see EBS in the tip box above). Or perhaps you're using one of those giant digital screens you can 'write' on and then save/print. Perhaps you're videoing the whole thing, because you're planning on showing an edit at the Christmas party.

Either way the point is the same: capturing the output of your sessions is really important. Yet so often, it's done very badly. Inaccurately. Incompletely.

This is such a basic mistake, but it's one I see again and again. People are coming up with brilliant ideas, but the person writing them up on the flipchart doesn't capture them properly. Either because they're rushing, or they don't understand what's being said, or they just don't personally like the idea.

All of which can be fatal for your ideation. If someone's idea is, 'Let people create looping, six-second videos that only record when their finger is touching the screen' but all that goes on the flipchart is 'short videos' then you've just lost the idea for Vine, Twitter's phenomenally successful video app.

So, here are three tips for creating notes that do justice to the ideas:

i. **Be disciplined.** Make sure you're accurately and completely capturing the ideas. Don't shortchange them, and don't filter them at this early stage. If people start throwing out multiple ideas simultaneously, pause to write them all up. If you're not the person recording the session, pick up if the person who is, isn't doing the ideas justice.

ii. **Be diligent.** As well as using a flipchart, you could have someone whose job it is not to participate, but to diligently and comprehensively capture the ideas in a notebook, to review later.

iii. **Be changeable.** Try changing the person who's writing up the ideas every time you change tool. It keeps things lively and means people can start to develop a shared 'best practice' way of getting the ideas down.

Anyway, before you can say, 'Where *has* the morning gone?' you realise you've stacked up a huge pile of life-changing, game-changing, rule-breaking, breath-taking ideas.

You may need to rivet the flipchart to the floor, it'll be vibrating so strongly with the potential energy you've poured into it. You're Pixar in that lunch meeting I mentioned right at the start. But just like Pixar, now you've got to put in the hard yards, developing those seed ideas into something more fully formed.

3.
Development

'Good, better, best. Never let it rest. Until your good is better and your better is best.' TIM DUNCAN

One idea will prove the spur for another.

Building on ideas, developing them, enhancing them, it can all happen during the session.

There's a belief that brainstorming should *only* be about getting the largest possible quantity of ideas – and of course that's important. But, while everyone's fired up and 'bouncing ideas off each other', it's invaluable to have people and ideas interact. *Idea A* may not cause someone else to come up with *Idea B*, but they may come up with *Idea A Ultra*.

The facilitator needs to find the right balance, which will depend on the speed of the session and the personalities involved. Some development and 'Oh yes, and what if ...' positive building is great – just watch out that the session doesn't get bogged down endlessly debating and refining one idea during the idea-generation process or lots of other potential winners will get lost.

But clearly, you're not going to finish a brainstorming session with every idea perfectly polished. After all, storms aren't really the best environment for polishing.

Having spent time thinking *up* ideas, you need to spend some time thinking *about* those ideas. It's time to push them, prod them, pull them apart and put them back together in better shape than they started.

Are they any good? Could they be better? Of course they could. Does spending a bit more time discussing one of them inspire someone to think of something stronger? In problem solving, $1 + 1 = 3$.

There are a number of routes you might choose for a development session:

1. The original group could work on them on the same day.

2. The original group could work on them at a later time.

3. A smaller group (a subset of the original) could develop them.

Getting the entire group to give up a whole day might be a big ask. The advantage of getting people to work on it the same day is that they still remember the ideas well and their brains are in a heightened state of creativity. The disadvantage is that you might all be mentally knackered.

In which case, schedule in a development session for a few days (no more than a week) later. Use an exercise like the movie poster icebreaker (perhaps developing a poster for one of the solutions you have, rather than of the problem again) or the 'Mad Inventor' described in tool ix, *random insertion*, to get everyone back into a creative, collaborative mindset.

It may be that you feel the whole group isn't needed (or efficacious) for developing ideas. That's OK; just bring in the people you feel are right – but try and maintain a bit of variety in personality and experience.

Whatever you do, you'll be going back to the flipchart and panning for gold.

Turning a good idea into a great one

Here are four suggestions for developing ideas further.

i. Distil not dilute

Remind everyone – as often as needed – that *development* isn't about trying to make a solution more palatable to the business. You're working with the aim of making the solution more potent. Don't worry, the desire to dilute will come from other people soon enough, when you get to *implementation*. But for now, work like idealists to push the idea on.

Do great business breakthroughs come about as a result of compromise and dilution and trying to please all of the people all of the time? No, of course not.

ii. Combine and refine

We've already talked about the idea of using multiple tools on one problem/opportunity not merely to try different ways of cracking the same starting point, but to try and take each step of progress on a little further. It may be that when you come to development sessions, you want to try this angle again.

For instance, give yourself a new *constraint*: how do we do this solution, but for half the price or in half the time? Or *think bigger*: could this idea be used in a broader context than we're currently considering?

> **PROBLEM-SOLVING TIP**
>
> As Leo Burnett said, 'When you reach for the stars you may not quite get one, but you won't come up with a handful of mud either.' What's the equivalent here? To take the idea you've got and push it to the *nth* degree; be really demanding of yourselves and say, 'How could this solution be amplified even more?' As Spinal Tap would say, turn it up to 11.

iii. Persistence beats resistance

A really important one this: just keep going. I've already said that a thinking tool can provide the 1 per cent inspiration, you need to provide the 99 per cent perspiration. So show some persistence: if you believe you've got the nugget of a great solution, keep discussing it, researching it, prodding it ... really work your brains and bounce 'What if' ideas off each other to take things further – beyond what your business has ever done before. Perhaps beyond what *anyone* has done before (especially if you're looking for a real innovation).

And be critical of yourselves: Are we going far enough? Are we thinking broad enough or deep enough? Be excited: how far could we take this? And as I say, be determined: we're not giving up 'til we've cracked it. Instead of saying, 'It doesn't quite work', make your mantra, 'It doesn't quite work ... yet'.

I'm back to Edison again and his famous quote, 'I have not failed. I've just found 10,000 ways that do not work.' Or Henry Ford, who when told he'd been lucky, replied, 'Yes, I have been lucky. And I find that the harder I work, the luckier I get.'

PROBLEM-SOLVING TIP

I've already mentioned spider diagrams in *interrogate and extrapolate*; they can be useful here too. Or try a digital version like the *MindNode* app. You've got your core new idea at the centre. Now when people come up with an addition or refinement, that becomes a new node off the centre. That new thought may inspire a comment from someone else – if it's related to the new node, then it comes off that one. But if it's just connected to the initial idea, it comes off that central node. That way you have a visual, at-a-glance representation of the relationship between – and relative scale of – each development.

Unlike the sequential nature of flipchart recording, spider diagrams can encourage the group to build on an area, rather than just adding to a list with a new, unrelated thought each time.

---

iv. Play angel's advocate as well as devil's advocate

I always think it's nice to play angel's advocate first. Ask: what do we like about our idea? What are its strengths? Try this: get everyone involved in *development* to say, in turn, something positive about the idea being discussed. What's a benefit of it? Go round the room several times – force people to keep coming up with new positives. For one thing, it'll give you a great list of 'selling points' when you want to get the idea implemented by the business – a list of benefits more comprehensive than you may have captured up until now.

But discussing benefits can also surprise people: a benefit that one person thought was obvious (so didn't previously mention) is something another person had never considered. But now they've heard it, it's given them another idea, or a thought to augment that benefit's effect.

Then, after the angel's advocacy, it's time for the stress testing. Ask what *isn't* great about the idea; what its shortcomings might be 'in the real world'.

You don't want to take the edge off (or lose enthusiasm for) your solution by getting too 'practical' too soon. But looking at it this way can be useful because now you're creating new, smaller problems – problems around implementation of your great idea. And since you're in a roomful of problem-solving experts at the top of their game, what better time to explore some of those problems. Tackling them might well make the initial idea even stronger.

PROBLEM-SOLVING TIP

I've seen it in advertising agencies many times: the client comes back with amends on your work, telling you there's such-and-such an issue with it. And the creatives groan and moan and curse the heavens. But then they go and work on the work to address the problem. And do you know what: often, afterwards, they'll grudgingly admit that the idea is now stronger than it was before.

Contributing after the session

At the end of the session(s), people will be tired, but (hopefully) buzzing. You've made great progress. In a day's work you've got further than you had in the previous six months. Time for a celebratory, restorative lunch.

But people's brains might keep working, even after the development. There might be an idea or two that particularly resonates with them. So at the end of any session, make it easy for people to add further thoughts later. Give them an email address. Email them the notes. Tell everyone you *want* them to say something more on the subject – that you want comments on the notes, particularly any other ideas/developments. Once people have had a few days to absorb the session and ruminate on it, what you might get back is just a collection of 'My favourite is number 3' or 'Number 4 will never work'. But you might just get back a little gem.

So make it clear: just because the problem-solving session is over, doesn't mean the problem solving is.

The session is the beginning. The successful implementation is the end. What happens in between is also important.

4.
Implementation

'The man with a new idea is a crank – until the idea succeeds.' MARK TWAIN

I'm sure *successful business implementation* could do with a (probably fairly dull) book of its own. I've worked at huge multinationals and at small independent companies and I've often been involved in trying to push great ideas through. And it's rarely, barely ever been easy.

I'd go as far as saying that often, getting an idea implemented is a bigger achievement than coming up with the idea in the first place. The world is full of brilliant scripts and songs and inventions that never made it out of someone's desk drawer. And the same is true of business solutions and innovations. There are many more in existence than get executed. Which is a terrible shame and a fantastic loss in income, productivity and competitiveness.

So the gazillion-dollar question is: how do you get your ideas off the flipchart, into the boardroom … and then into the business?

If I had a definitive answer, I'd be a gazillionaire. Very often it can be very difficult. Look back at some of the examples in this book and you'll see that many of the solutions and innovations came from the top. Steve Jobs. Michael O'Leary. James Dyson. Not always, but it helps. Therefore I'd suggest that if you're the CEO of your business then you're going to find *implementation* a doddle, assuming you can garner the necessary resources.

For everyone else, the biggest barrier is usually other people: persuading those who need to sign off on the idea, and galvanising those who need to be involved in its execution. Here are five tips that may help you win over both groups.

i. Collaborate as you innovate

I mentioned this in the *preparation* section. Get the decision makers involved in the process – make them feel part of the ideation – and they're much more likely to sign-off on it. Get the people who will be affected by the change involved in shaping it and they're much more likely to embrace it too. Don't present your idea as a *fait accompli* to either group. Invite their feedback; it may improve the idea and it should improve their affection for it.

ii. Develop a proof of concept

'Proof of concept' means showing in miniature – like a prototype or a small-scale 'live' test or a working model – that your idea is a goer. Before the movie *Sin City* was made, they developed a proof of concept; a short piece of film demonstrating that the green screen technique they wanted to use would work. (In fact, the short they produced ended up becoming the prologue in the finished movie.) How would you do a proof of concept for your idea? Or what's the closest you can get to one, to demonstrate and 'prove' that your idea has a great chance of success and de-risk things for the decision makers?

> **PROBLEM-SOLVING TIP**
>
> 'It's easier to ask forgiveness than permission.' You could just go ahead with your proof of concept as a small-scale live test and film it (if appropriate) or invite the decision maker to come see it in action. Rather than try to get someone to give the go-ahead after seeing a conventional presentation of the theory, get them to agree to just scale up the live demo that you've already shown is working.

iii. Stress test

It's not great for anyone involved to be in a conversation where one person says, 'I've got a great idea here', the other person says, 'What about issues *X*, *Y* and *Z*?' and the first person says, 'Err … Oh.'

You must run your devil's advocate session in advance, to identify any challenges to your idea and establish whether or not they're real, if not why not, and if they're genuine how you'd overcome them.

It's important to show you've done your research and it's important to have an informed, considered answer ready for whatever criticism may come your idea's way. Don't wing it.

iv. Prepare your pitch

I think it was Abraham Lincoln who said something along the lines of, 'When I am preparing to speak to someone, I spend twice as long thinking about what they want to hear as I do on what I want to say.' Five quick tips for making a strong pitch:

(a) What's the headline?

You need a hook – a single-minded, memorable headline story for your solution/innovation. Online it's called 'link baiting' – devising a headline that draws people in. 'Why the world will end on October the 14th.' 'Eight reasons you need to starting eating kidney beans NOW.' 'What this little girl said to made the president cry.' 'Lose ten pounds in a week with this one weird tip.' Look at the way some blog links compose their headlines to see how to come up with a powerful hook to summarise your idea.

Even a catchy name can help. Like 'WiFi'. We all use the term and we all know what it means. Yet no one I've met knows what it actually stands for. It just rhymes. If 'Wi' is *wireless*, what's 'Fi'?

(b) Facts and figures

Go back to the list of benefits you did in the 'angel's advocate' exercise in *development*. That list is going to be really useful here. And people find figures very compelling: can you monetise any of the benefits? Assign them a percentage increase in customer satisfaction? Show it will save an annual pile of paperwork as high as the Gherkin? Increase your market share by eight points?

(c) Face to face

Don't just email your idea; arrange a meeting to discuss it face to face. Rehearse your presentation, make it memorable and be sure to arrange a follow-up meeting. Don't just leave the idea with them, hoping they'll action it; at the end of the first meeting, agree when you'll meet up again to discuss your proposal further. The next step should always be either implementation or another meeting. Never just, 'I'll get back to you'.

(d) Find something analogous

Is there anyone else, in any other market, who's used a similar approach to the one you're suggesting, with great success? It may be worth presenting it, again to help de-risk the *implementation* in the eyes of the decision makers.

A word of disclosure here: in psychology this is known as 'confirmation bias' – finding a case study that fits your hypothesis and discounting examples that would seem to undermine it. Just because someone else seemed to have success with *solution A*, doesn't mean you will. In truth there are probably thousands of variables involved in their success which you just can't calculate. The timeliness for one thing – perhaps there was something unique about the time when they implemented their strategy that you can't replicate because the world's moved on since then.

But this isn't about saying, 'If we copy such-and-such a company we'll definitely get the same result they did'. It's about showing that what you're proposing maybe isn't as 'out there' and untried as it might first appear – and so maybe isn't as risky as it might first appear.

(e) Make it easy

Sometimes people can have the attitude of, 'I came up with the idea, now it's your job to implement it'. Those are people whose ideas live in the neglected, forgotten bottom drawer of a middle manager's desk in a grey office block on an industrial estate.

Because if what you're doing is having a meeting basically saying, 'I've come up with a great idea . . . that's going to mean a lot of work for you to implement and it'll hoover up your budget and there's no guarantee of success but if it does work then I'm taking all the glory' ... well, you wouldn't be surprised if they just smiled thinly and showed you the door.

Think about it from their point of view. If you were them, what would persuade you? First of all, because it was easy to say yes to: because the person who'd had the idea was willing to take on the task and responsibility of making it happen. In fact, they'd already done a lot of the leg work and got the fundamentals in place.

v. Persistence beats resistance, part 2

Here's a quote from a LinkedIn piece ('How to Create Success By Being Ruthlessly Focused', November 2013) by multi-millionaire businessman James Caan of *Dragons' Den*: 'I was once giving a talk at a university when I was approached by somebody who wanted to work for me. Although he didn't necessarily have the experience, he was very persistent and driven. One day he turned up at my office unannounced, and it was clear he was determined to work for me. I ended up creating a role within the business for him, and then a couple of years later he pitched me a brilliant business idea. Now he runs an entire portfolio of investments.'

We all know history is littered with examples of people who refused to take no for an answer, who just kept going (like J. K. Rowling, who was not only rejected by the first 12 publishers to see her manuscript, but apparently the publisher who took it on told her to get a day job as she'd never make a living writing children's books).

Just as you've got to keep going in *development*, so in *implementation*. Persevere. If your idea – whether it solves a problem, capitalises on an opportunity or inspires innovation – really is good, then eventually someone will see in it what you did in your *generation* and *development* sessions.

Like I said before, the story of how James Dyson was turned down by every vacuum cleaner manufacturer he approached is now famous. But why is it famous? Only because he kept going and proved them wrong. If, after they'd all turned him down, he'd given up then we'd never have heard of him. And I'd still have a vacuum cleaner (with a bag) that loses suction.

Or here's Lincoln again, this time with a quote that's the antithesis of the famous Guinness slogan. 'Things may come to those who wait. But only the things left by those who hustle.'

It also reminds me of a poster I once saw doing the email rounds. It was just typographic and said (using somewhat fruitier language), 'Some days I feel like giving up. But then I remember just how many people I have to prove wrong'.

In conclusion:
a better answer

'I was gratified to be able to answer promptly, and I did. I said I didn't know.' MARK TWAIN

Solving problems can be extremely enjoyable.

Seizing on opportunities can be extremely rewarding.

Innovating means people start referring to you as 'Brains'.

And there's always a better answer out there.

The cleaners at a school complained to the head that students using the girls' toilets were leaving lipstick kisses on the mirrors. They'd put up notices asking them to stop but that hadn't worked. If anything, the problem was getting worse. And the grease in lipstick meant it was a pain to remove, day after day.

So the head called a group of girls, as representatives, to the toilets. She pointed out the lipstick kisses on the mirror. Many of the girls couldn't hide their smiles.

'Removing lipstick isn't easy,' said the head. 'It's designed to stay on your lips, after all. So wiping it off every day is something of a problem.'

A couple of girls sniggered.

'Luckily, we've found an effective method that we'll be using from now on,' said the head. And the cleaner who was with her took a sponge, dipped it into the toilet bowl ... and wiped the mirrors with it.

The lipstick problem disappeared overnight.

I hope you found the background in *Insight* interesting and the session tips in *Inspiration* useful. But most of all, I hope you find the 12 creative thinking tools of *Innovation* to be boons you'll turn to again and again.

I've worked with banks, technology companies, car companies, tourism companies, food companies and charities. All felt their problems were unique. Yet the methods for solving their problems were common to all. And they're all in this book.

PROBLEM-SOLVING TIP

Think positively, be enthused and generate energy. Believe in yourself, believe in the team. Know that you are creative and you will succeed. Keep things stimulating (important), maintain focus (very important), and give yourselves time out to let your brains reflect on what you've done (really important). And remember: there is *always* a better answer out there. It has not 'all been done'. Just adopt the attitude of the world's most famous Belgian.

'What other explanation can there be?' Poirot stared straight ahead of him. 'That is what I ask myself,' he said. 'That is what I never cease to ask myself.' (Agatha Christie, *Murder on the Orient Express*)

And, as I've said before, these tools will be dynamite for *your* ideation too. Dynamite that's been dipped in popping candy, wrapped in Semtex and tied to a firework.

So, there we are. Let me finish with one more story, of how Gandhi turned a problem into an opportunity.

He was getting on a train when his shoe came off, falling down the gap between the train and the platform. He couldn't retrieve it ...

... so he took off his other shoe and dropped it down after the first one. His travelling companions looked at him somewhat confused. At which point Gandhi explained that a poor person who finds a single shoe is no better off.

What's really helpful is finding a pair.

Best of luck with your problem solving and bear in mind the words of André Gide: 'Man cannot discover new oceans unless he has the courage to lose sight of the shore.' And next time you achieve a tremendous breakthrough using the tools in this book, please let me know at thinking.tools@icloud.com. And cut me in.

Recommended reading

Every now and then I mentioned other books that could tell you more than I have. Here's the list all brought together.

Barden, Phil, *Decoded*, John Wiley & Sons, 2013.

Baron, Renee and Wagele, Elizabeth, *The Enneagram Made Easy: Discover the 9 Types of People*, Thorsons, 1994.

De Bono, Edward, *Lateral Thinking: A Textbook of Creativity*, Penguin, 2009.

Eagleman, David, *Incognito: The Secret Lives of the Brain*, Canongate, 2012.

Gladwell, Malcolm, *The Tipping Point*, new edn, Abacus, 2002.

Goleman, Daniel, *Emotional Intelligence: Why it Can Matter More than IQ*, Bloomsbury, 1996.

Hargadon, Andrew, *How Breakthroughs Happen*, Harvard Business School Press, 2003.

Hartwell, Margaret and Chen, Joshua, *Archetypes in Branding: A Toolkit for Creatives and Strategists*, How Design Books, 2012.

Kahneman, Daniel, *Thinking, Fast and Slow*, Penguin, 2012.

Lehrer, Jonah, *The Decisive Moment*, Canongate, 2012.

Lehrer, Jonah, *Imagine: How Creativity Works*, Houghton Mifflin Harcourt, 2012.

Morgan, Adam, *Eating the Big Fish*, 2nd edn, John Wiley & Sons, 2009.

Osborn, Alex, *Applied Imagination: Principles and Procedures of Creative Problem-Solving*, 3rd edn, revised, Charles Scribner's Sons, 1979.

Ramachandran, V. S., *The Tell-Tale Brain: Unlocking the Mystery of Human Nature*, Windmill Books, 2012.

Thaler, Richard H. and Sunstein, Cass R., *Nudge: Improving Decisions about Health, Wealth and Happiness*, Penguin, 2009.

Young, James Webb, *A Technique For Producing Ideas*, new edn, McGraw-Hill, 2003.

Index